Just-in-Time
for Healthcare

Lean Tools for Healthcare Series

Series Editor: Thomas L. Jackson

PUBLISHED

5S for Healthcare

Standard Work for Lean Healthcare

Kaizen Workshops for Lean Healthcare

Mapping Clinical Value Streams

Mistake Proofing for Lean Healthcare

FORTHCOMING

Just-in-Time for Healthcare

Continuous Flow for Healthcare

Quick Setup for Healthcare

Kanban for Healthcare

Just-in-Time
for Healthcare

Rona Consulting Group & Productivity Press
Thomas L. Jackson, Editor

CRC Press
Taylor & Francis Group
Boca Raton London New York

CRC Press is an imprint of the
Taylor & Francis Group, an **informa** business
A PRODUCTIVITY PRESS BOOK

CRC Press
Taylor & Francis Group
6000 Broken Sound Parkway NW, Suite 300
Boca Raton, FL 33487-2742

© 2017 by Taylor & Francis Group, LLC
CRC Press is an imprint of Taylor & Francis Group, an Informa business

No claim to original U.S. Government works

Printed on acid-free paper
Version Date: 20160917

International Standard Book Number-13: 978-1-4398-3745-0 (Paperback)

Library of Congress Cataloging-in-Publication Data

Names: Jackson, Thomas Lindsay, 1949- editor.
Title: Just-in-time for healthcare / Thomas L. Jackson.
Other titles: Lean tools for healthcare series.
Description: Boca Raton : Taylor & Francis, 2017. | Series: Lean tools for healthcare series
Identifiers: LCCN 2016038558 | ISBN 9781439837450 (pbk. : alk. paper) | ISBN 9781439837467 (eBook)
Subjects: | MESH: Health Facility Administration | Workflow | Efficiency, Organizational | Delivery of Health Care--economics | United States
Classification: LCC RA971 | NLM WX 150 AA1 | DDC 362.1068--dc23
LC record available at https://lccn.loc.gov/2016038558

Visit the Taylor & Francis Web site at
http://www.taylorandfrancis.com

and the CRC Press Web site at
http://www.crcpress.com

Contents

Preface

Just-in-time is an approach that can dramatically boost your healthcare organization's capability to eliminate waste from processes, serve patients more effectively, improve access, and reduce costs. *Just-in-time means producing the quality services patients require—when they need them, where they need them, and in just the amount they need.* It is a core element of any Lean production system, and in fact has come to be used as another word for Lean.

The change from traditional ways of producing and managing healthcare services to a just-in-time approach requires a new understanding about what adds value for the patient or customer, and what does not. This book is intended to share powerful knowledge that will help you participate effectively in the change to just-in-time.

As you read this book, you will realize that just-in-time is not really one approach, but rather a set of integrated approaches that supports a different way of operating. *Just-in-Time for Healthcare* provides an overview of waste and improvement in the operations and processes of healthcare (Chapter 2). It then introduces the main concepts of just-in-time, why it is so important for healthcare, and how it is implemented.

Next, the book addresses the concept of *flow* (the elimination of waits and delays from processes)—from the critical foundation of standard work, to process layouts that facilitate flow, to the importance of mistake proofing. You will then learn how individual areas, or *islands*, of flow are connected using the concept of pull. *Kanban* (signaling) methods are introduced, as well as the concept of *leveling* (the scheduling of service production to smoothen day-to-day variation and balance capacity with demand). The role of the *flow manager* is also introduced.

The book also briefly covers some of the support techniques that make just-in-time possible, including the *5S system for workplace organization, visual management techniques, mistake proofing, quick setup, new performance measures, and the five principles of Lean management.*

It is important to remember that this material is a general orientation to a complex topic. The implementation and mastery of the comprehensive just-in-time approach requires a deeper understanding of Lean production in health-care, best obtained through experiential learning and application with the help of a sensei—someone who has gone and done before you. Some further resources for learning are also listed in the Appendix.

One of the most effective ways to use this book is to read and discuss it with others in group learning sessions. We have planned the book so that it is easy to use in this way, with chunks of information that can be covered in a series of short sessions. Each chapter includes reflection questions to stimulate group discussion.

The just-in-time approach is universal. Today, the basic principles of just-in-time have been used to eliminate waste in all types of industries, and they are being put to work in healthcare organizations all over the world. We hope this book will show you how just-in-time can make your workplace better and safer for both patients and staff.

Acknowledgments

The development of *Just-in-Time for Healthcare* has been a team effort. In particular, I would like to acknowledge the Rona Consulting Group consultants who have contributed to our facilitation and coaching of just-in-time (JIT) implementation in our clients' organizations. Special thanks to Dr. James H. Hanson, who enriched the book with his insights. Thanks also to the team at Productivity Press and CRC Press, especially to Kristine Mednansky, senior editor.

I also acknowledge the many talented people of the Productivity Press Development Team who created the original book, *Just-in-Time for Operators* (1998), upon which much of this book is based. Cartoon illustrations in Figures 4.5 and 5.1 were created by Hannah Bonner.

Finally, we acknowledge the good work of the many doctors, nurses, technicians, administrators, and executives who are now in the process of implementing the JIT system in their own organizations. We are very pleased to bring you this addition to our Lean Tools for Healthcare Series and wish you continued and increasing success on your Lean journey.

Chapter 1

Getting Started

1.1 PURPOSE OF THIS BOOK

Just-in-Time for Healthcare was written to give you the information you need to participate in implementing this important Lean healthcare approach in your workplace. You are a valued member of your healthcare organization's transformation team; your knowledge, support, and participation are necessary to the success of any major improvement effort in your organization.

You may be reading this book because your team leader or manager asked you to do so. Or you may be reading it because you think it will provide information that will help you in your work. By the time you finish Chapter 1, you will have a better idea of how the information in this book can help you and your healthcare organization eliminate waste and serve your patients more effectively.

1.2 WHAT THIS BOOK IS BASED ON

BACKGROUND INFO This book is about the just-in-time (JIT) system that is fundamental to providing Lean healthcare services and eliminating waste from healthcare processes. In fact, JIT is another way of saying *Lean*. The methods and goals discussed in this book support the Lean healthcare system, which is based on a production and management system developed at Toyota Motor Company. Since 1979, Productivity Press has published knowledge and information about these approaches. Since 2007, Rona Consulting Group has been applying the knowledge in healthcare. Today, top organizations around the world are applying

Lean healthcare principles to improve patient experience, safety, quality, wait times, and affordability.

Just-in-Time for Healthcare draws on a wide variety of resources (see the Appendix for further information). Its aim is to present the main concepts and steps of JIT in a simple, illustrated format that is easy to read and understand.

1.3 TWO WAYS TO USE THIS BOOK

There are at least two ways to use this book:

1. As reading material for a learning group or study group process within your organization.
2. For learning on your own.

Your organization may decide to design its own learning group process based on *Just-in-Time for Healthcare*. Or, you may read this book for individual learning without formal group discussion. Either way, you will learn valuable concepts and methods to apply in your daily work.

1.4 HOW TO GET THE MOST OUT OF YOUR READING

1.4.1 Become Familiar with This Book as a Whole

There are a few steps you can follow to make it easier to absorb the information in this book. Take as much time as you need to become familiar with the material. First, get a *big-picture* view of the book by doing the following:

1. Scan the Contents to see how *Just-in-Time for Healthcare* is arranged.
2. Read the rest of this chapter for an overview of the book's contents.
3. Flip through the book to get a feel for its style, flow, and design. Notice how the chapters are structured and glance at the illustrations.

1.4.2 Become Familiar with Each Chapter

For each chapter in *Just-in-Time for Healthcare*, we suggest you follow these steps to get the most from your reading:

1. Flip through the chapter, looking at the way it is presented. Notice the bold headings and the key points flagged in the margins.
2. Read the chapter; enhance your reading by doing the following:
   a. Use the margin assists to help you follow the flow of information.
   b. If the book is your own, use a highlighter to mark key information and answers to your questions about the material. If the book is not your own, take notes on a separate piece of paper.
   c. Answer the *Take Five* questions in the text. These will help you absorb the information by reflecting on how you might apply it to your own workplace.
3. Read the summary at the end of the chapter to reinforce what you have learned. If you do not remember something in the summary, find that section in the chapter and review it.
4. Finally, read the *Reflections* questions at the end of the chapter. Think about these questions and write down your answers.

1.4.3 Use a Reading Strategy

When reading a book, many people think they should start with the first word and read straight through to the end. This is not usually the best way to learn from a book. The method described here is easier and more effective.

A reading strategy is based on two simple points about the way people learn. The first point is this: *It is difficult for your brain to absorb new information if it does not have a structure in which to place it*. As an analogy, imagine trying to build a house without first putting up a framework.

Like building a frame for a house, you can give your brain a framework for the new information in the book by getting an overview of the contents and then flipping through the material. Within each chapter, you repeat this process on a smaller scale by reading the key points and headings before reading the text.

The second point about learning is this: *It is a lot easier to learn if you take in the information one layer at a time instead of trying to absorb it all at once.* It is like finishing the walls of a house: First, you lay down a coat of primer. When that is dry, you apply a coat of paint and later a finish coat.

1.4.4 Use the Margin Assists

As you have noticed by now, this book uses small images called *margin assists* to help you follow the information in each chapter. There are seven types of margin assists:

1. *Background Information:* Sets the stage for what comes next.

2. *Definition:* Defines important words.

3. *Key Point:* Highlights important ideas to remember.

4. *Example:* Helps you understand the key points.

5. *New Tool:* Helps you apply what you have learned.

6. *How-To Steps:* Gives you a set of directions for using new tools.

7. *Principle:* Explains how things work in a variety of situations.

1.5 OVERVIEW OF THE CONTENTS

1.5.1 Chapter 1: Getting Started

The chapter you are reading explains the purpose of *Just-in-Time for Healthcare* and how it was written. It gives tips for getting the most out of your reading and provides an overview of each chapter.

1.5.2 Chapter 2: The Production Processes and Operations of Healthcare

Chapter 2 describes the industrial origins of the Lean healthcare methodology and discusses the concept of waste in healthcare. It also defines the critical distinction between healthcare processes and operations.

1.5.3 Chapter 3: An Introduction to Just-in-Time

Chapter 3 introduces and defines *just-in-time*. It explains why it is important and the benefits of JIT for you and your organization. Finally, it covers the five phases of changing to a JIT system for producing healthcare services.

1.5.4 Chapter 4: Creating Islands of Flow

In Chapter 4, you will learn how *flow* is established in discrete healthcare production units called cells. We create flow when we eliminate waits and delays so that patients move smoothly through a process that is perfectly synchronized with the actual demand for services. This chapter also covers the basic concepts of *standard work*—the foundation for JIT.

1.5.5 Chapter 5: Using Pull to Connect Islands of Flow

Chapter 5 explains how JIT teams and cells are connected in a system called *pull*. Pull systems are defined and then contrasted with the typical *push* production systems used in healthcare. The chapter covers the basics of the *kanban*, or signaling, systems that are used to transform the continuum of care into a pull system. Finally, it explains how a *flow manager* adjusts the schedule in real time to keep it in sync with actual demand.

1.5.6 Chapter 6: Support Techniques for Just-in-Time

This chapter describes several important techniques that support the smooth flow required for JIT in healthcare. These include the *5S system* for workplace organization and standardization, *visual management* techniques, *mistake proofing*, *quick setup* methods, and healthcare performance measures that reinforce JIT. It also outlines the five key principles of Lean healthcare management.

1.5.7 Chapter 7: Reflections and Conclusions

Chapter 7 presents brief reflections and conclusions for this book. It also describes opportunities for additional learning about JIT, which are further detailed in the Appendix.

Chapter 2

The Production Processes and Operations of Healthcare

2.1 THE INDUSTRIAL ORIGINS OF LEAN HEALTHCARE

Just-in-Time for Healthcare is a succinct overview of the core methods of Lean healthcare that are explored in more detail in other titles in the Lean Tools for Healthcare Series. The purpose of the series is to introduce readers to a set of methods that have been proven to dramatically increase patient safety and reduce the cost of providing healthcare services. The term *Lean* is another way to say *just-in-time* (JIT). It was coined to express the notion that, like an athlete, an organization should be without organizational *fat* or what Lean specialists refer to as non-value-adding waste, where value refers to what a patient would be willing to pay for. Figure 2.1 lists seven distinct types of waste found in healthcare.

Lean or JIT tools and methods have important origins in the United States but were perfected principally within the Toyota Motor Company between 1948 and 1963, and have since been adopted by most sectors of the manufacturing industry. The first major implementation in the healthcare industry began in 2001, when the Virginia Mason Medical Center in Seattle, Washington, engaged consultants (most of whom had been production engineers from Toyota and the Boeing Aircraft Company) to teach them how to apply the Toyota Production System

Seven wastes in healthcare operations and administration		
Definitions	Healthcare wastes	Administrative wastes
1. Overproduction Producing more, sooner, or faster than is required by the next process.	Performing services that patients don't need or desire. Unnecessary backups between departments. Multiple quality control checks.	Printing or processing reports, emails, or other information products before they are needed. Overdissemination of reports.
2. Waiting Time delays, process idle time.	Waiting for lab results. Waiting for doctors. Waiting for nurses. Waiting for patients. Waiting for decisions from hospital administrators. Idle people.	Searching for information. Waiting for information system response. Waiting for approvals from superiors.
3. Transportation Unnecessary handling or transportation; multiple handling.	Excessive medical record pickups and deliveries. Extra hand-offs. Excess patient transfer/ movement.	Transferring data files between incompatible computer systems or software packages. Over-dissemination of reports.
4. Overprocessing Unnecessary processing, steps, or work elements/ procedures.	Asking the patient the same question 20 times. Multiple signatures. Extra copies of same form. Duplicate data input entries.	Re-entering data, extra copies; reformatting or excessive/custom formatting. Unnecessary reviews. CCs on emails.
5. Inventory Producing, holding or purchasing unnecessary inventory.	Cabinets full of gloves. Piles of paper forms. Too many suture materials. Too many prosthetic devices. Multiple storage sites.	Decisions in process. Outdated, obsolete information in file cabinets or stored in databases.
6. Motion Excessive handling, unnecessary steps, nonergonomic motion.	Long reaches/walk distances. Lifting more than 35 pounds. Standing all day. Sitting all day. Not enough printers. Not enough copiers.	Repetitive stress injuries resulting from poor keyboard design. Excessive walking to and from remote printers.
7. Defects Rework, correction of errors, quality problems, equipment problems.	Adverse events. High infection rates. Wrong meds. Wrong surgical site. Frequent rescheduling. Patient readmissions.	Order-entry errors. Too many bill rejects. Design errors and engineering change orders. Invoice errors. Info system downtime.

Figure 2.1 Seven wastes. (From J. Michael Rona and Associates, LLC, doing business as Rona Consulting Group © 2008–2016. All rights reserved. Reprinted with permission.)

to the production of healthcare services. A few years later, another major implementation was launched by Park Nicollet Health Services in Minneapolis, and a few other organizations, including Thedacare in Wisconsin. The success of these implementations is well documented.*

---

* Black, John and David Miller. 2008. *The Toyota Way to Healthcare Excellence: Increase Efficiency and Improve Quality with Lean.* Chicago: Health Administration Press.

Naturally, readers coming to the subject of JIT for the first time are often perplexed by the patently industrial point of view taken by Lean healthcare specialists. How can healthcare be treated as an industrial process? Isn't medicine an art? Can healthcare processes be standardized when all patients are unique? In fact, medicine and healthcare practice are generally becoming more scientific or evidence based, and the Centers for Medicare & Medicaid Services and deeming authorities such as the Joint Commission are quick to require adherence to standardized, evidence-based practices. Moreover, industrial engineering has long been applied to healthcare processes. Some readers may recall actor Clifton Webb's portrayal of the time-and-motion consultant Frank Gilbreth in the movie, *Cheaper by the Dozen*. The movie depicts Gilbreth's ground-breaking time and motion studies of surgery in hospital operating rooms. In many ways, the practice of Lean healthcare continues in the tradition of Gilbreth's time studies. The critical difference is that the studies are not carried out by consultants; the studies and improvement work are conducted by members of the healthcare team (clinicians and support staff), frequently with the voluntary participation of patients themselves.

2.1.1 How Much Waste Is There in Healthcare?

How much waste is there in healthcare today? In a recent *Journal of the American Medical Association* (*JAMA*) article, it was reported that, in 2011, wasted expenditures on healthcare in the United States totaled between $558 billion and $1,263 billion. The money was consumed by the following:

- Failures (defects) in care delivery
- Failures (defects) in care coordination
- Overtreatment
- Administrative complexity
- Pricing failures
- Fraud and abuse

Of the wastes cited in the *JAMA* article, all but pricing failures, fraud, and abuse can probably be explained in terms of the seven deadly wastes listed in Figure 2.1. Of these seven, two wastes are the most obvious to the casual observer: (1) waiting and (2) defects. In 2011, the low estimate—$558 billion—represented 17.5% of all spending on healthcare in the United States. By 2020, this figure is expected to rise to over 20%.*

2.1.2 Waiting Is Waste

Throughout healthcare, one can see patients waiting: waiting to be seen by their clinicians, waiting for an appointment, waiting to be admitted, waiting for a room, waiting to be taken to the bathroom, waiting for lab results, or waiting to be discharged. All of this waiting extends time in the clinic, time in the lab, and lengths of stay in the hospital. The implications for patient satisfaction are obvious. It increases the cost of healthcare and, in the case of long hospital stays, increases the risk of deadly hospital-acquired infections. It also reduces access to healthcare by other patients in the population because valuable capacity is currently occupied.

 Another type of waiting, almost invisible unless you know how to look for it, is present in the form of interruptions. Nurses, physicians, and their support staff are constantly interrupted by pagers, text messages, emails, phone calls, call lights, hospital codes, and questions from patients and families and of course by waiting for patients, for other clinicians and staff, for reports, for lab results, and so on. Although each interruption may only require a few minutes or even seconds, such interruptions take their toll.

The sum of all the time wasted on interruptions is a problem; extra time costs money. In manufacturing, where a similar problem exists in the form of small but constant interruptions in equipment performance, significant time and energy are devoted to improving equipment to ensure smooth production flow.

---

* Berwick, Donald M. and Andrew Hackbarth. 2012. Eliminating waste in U.S. healthcare. *JAMA*, Vol. 307, No. 14, pp. 1513–1516, April 11.

In healthcare, there is even more at stake. Recent studies in the field of *interruption science* show that, once distracted, workers can take more than 20 minutes to get *back into the groove*. While clinicians and staff members may pride themselves on their ability to multitask, the science shows that multitasking is an illusion. The human brain is simply not designed to deal with constant changes in the context of decision making. The implications for productivity in the healthcare industry are staggering, not to mention the implications for clinical quality and patient safety. By eliminating interruptions (and other wastes), JIT helps healthcare stay focused—on the patient.

2.1.3 Defects Are Waste

Defects—specifically, failures in care delivery and coordination—are an obvious form of waste. *Defects compromise clinical quality and put patient safety at risk.* In healthcare, we have known for over a decade that poor quality is epidemic. Recent studies indicate that there are between 210,000 and 440,000 unnecessary deaths from avoidable medical errors in U.S. hospitals. The number would rise to far more shocking proportions if we included physical and mental harm in the equation. While many of these defects are inadvertent, the causes are deeply rooted in the culture of healthcare. *The New York Times* has reported that only one out of seven defects and accidents that harm Medicare patients is recognized and reported. Clearly, this makes it difficult to analyze, understand, and prevent defects in the future.[*,†]

2.2 PRODUCTION, PROCESS, AND OPERATION

Before studying the JIT system of Lean healthcare, you must understand precisely how the notion of *production* applies

---

[*] Allen, Marshall. How many die from medical mistakes in U.S. hospitals. *ProPublica*, Sep. 19. Available at http://www.propublica.org/article/how-many -die-from-medical-mistakes-in-us-hospitals.

[†] Pear, Robert. 2012. Report finds most errors at hospitals go unreported. *The New York Times*, January 6. Available at http://www.nytimes.com/2012/01/06 /health/study-of-medicare-patients-finds-most-hospital-errors-unreported.html.

to the production of healthcare services.* As perplexing as it may seem, production is not necessarily an activity that requires machines.

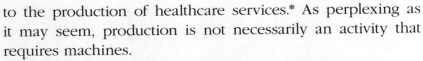 *Production is the making of either a product or a service—it does not matter which.*

Obviously, artisans produced goods and services before the advent of steam power. In its most general sense, production is simply a network of what industrial engineers call processes and operations.

A process is a sequence of cycles of work called "operations." An operation is a work cycle defined by a sequence of component tasks.

Figure 2.2 illustrates how a healthcare process—transforming a patient from the state of *unhealthy* to *healthy*—is accomplished through a series of medical and other healthcare operations. When we look at a healthcare process over time (especially when we see it from the patient's perspective), we see flows of patients, clinicians, medicines, supplies, equipment, and information in time and space. We see the transformation of the patient from the moment at which he or she presents undiagnosed symptoms, to initial assessment, definitive diagnosis, and finally treatment and recovery. When we look at operations, on the other hand, we see the work performed by doctors, nurses, lab technicians, pharmacists, and so on to accomplish this transformation—the interaction of patients, clinicians, medications, information, supplies, and equipment in time and space.

To make fundamental improvement in the production of healthcare services, we must distinguish the flow of patients (process) from the clinical workflow (operations) and analyze them separately. This is why Figure 2.2 illustrates healthcare production as a network of processes and operations. The analysis of healthcare *processes* examines the flow of patients; the analysis of healthcare *operations* examines the work performed on patients by clinicians and support staff.

---

* Much of this chapter paraphrases, in language friendly to healthcare, Chapter 1 of Shigeo Shingo's groundbreaking book, *A Study of the Toyota Production System from an Industrial Engineering Perspective* (Cambridge, MA: Productivity Press, 1989).

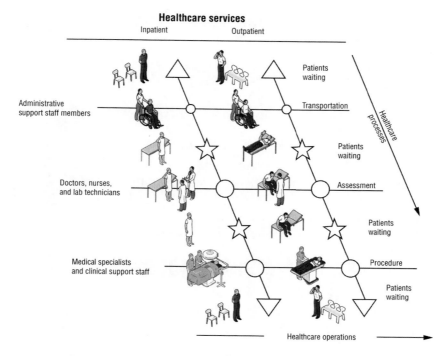

Healthcare services

Figure 2.2 Healthcare service production process. (From J. Michael Rona and Associates, LLC, doing business as Rona Consulting Group, and iStockphoto LP, © 2008–2016. All rights reserved. Reprinted with permission.)

Consider a typical patient who makes a visit to an outpatient clinic: First, the patient is registered at the front desk and then asked to wait. Next, a medical assistant calls the patient and escorts him or her to an examination room. The medical assistant may take the patient's blood pressure and ask questions to make an initial assessment of the patient's condition. Again, the patient is asked to wait until the doctor is ready. Finally, the doctor interviews the patient and reaches a diagnosis. After this, the patient receives some treatment—say, an injection administered by a nurse, who first draws the prescribed medication and, after cleaning the patient's injection site, injects the medication into the patient. This series of changes in the patient (from undiagnosed to treated) is the process. The nurse's actions of filling the syringe, cleaning the patient's injection site, and injecting the medication into the patient constitute a single operation within the process. In the healthcare industry, such operations are often referred to as *protocols.*

TAKE FIVE

Take a few minutes to think about these questions and to write down your answers:

- What kinds of processes happen in your work area?
- What kinds of operations do you perform in your daily work?

2.3 IMPROVING PROCESSES, AS WELL AS OPERATIONS

Since operations involve actions performed on patients, operational improvements often focus on the specific way actions are carried out. Improving operations might, for example, involve adjusting the location of medicines, supplies, and tools to reduce walking by clinicians.

 To improve production, however, it is not enough to improve operations. In implementing JIT, an organization must also improve its processes. Process improvements actually eliminate or reduce non-value-adding operations that hold up the flow between operations. This means finding ways to reduce delays, transport, mistakes, defects, and other situations that stop the flow of patients.

In JIT, patients pass smoothly through the process, ideally one at a time. The rest of this book describes the mechanics of JIT and the types of waste-eliminating improvements in operations and processes that make this smooth flow possible in healthcare.

SUMMARY

The term "Lean" is another way to say just-in-time. It was coined to express the notion that, like an athlete, an organization should be without organizational fat or what Lean specialists refer to as non-value-adding waste, where value refers to what a patient would be willing to pay for. Enormous waste exists in healthcare, including the waste of waiting and the waste of defects in care delivery and coordination. By eliminating waste in its many forms, JIT helps healthcare stay focused— on the patient.

All production, whether carried out in any healthcare setting—in the operating room, the clinic, the lab, or the pharmacy—must be understood as a functional network of processes and operations. Healthcare processes transform unwell patients into well patients. Healthcare operations are the clinical actions that accomplish those transformations. These fundamental concepts and their relationship must be understood in order to make effective, evidence-based improvements in the production of healthcare services.

In implementing JIT, an organization improves processes, as well as operations. Process improvements include finding ways to reduce delays, storage, transport, mistakes, defects, and other situations that stop the flow.

REFLECTIONS

Now that you have completed this chapter, take a few minutes to think about these questions and write down your answers:

- What did you learn from reading this chapter that stands out as being particularly useful or interesting to you in healthcare?
- How do you feel about the idea of *producing* healthcare services using industrial methods?
- Do you have any questions about the topics presented in this chapter? If so, what are they?
- Are there any special obstacles in your mind or the minds of your colleagues to applying the distinction between process and operation in healthcare?
- What information do you still need to understand fully the ideas presented?
- How can you get this information?
- Whom do you need to involve in this process?

Chapter 3

An Introduction to Just-in-Time

3.1 WHAT IS JUST-IN-TIME?

Just-in-time (often called JIT for short) is an approach that enables a healthcare organization to efficiently and reliably produce the quality services its patients require— when they need them, where they need them, and in the amount they need. Because the approach was first pioneered in manufacturing at the Toyota Motor Company, JIT is also known as the *Toyota Production System (TPS)*. More recently, JIT has become commonly known as *Lean production* because JIT systems are capable of producing the same output with far fewer resources.*

JIT or Lean production differs from the traditional approach to producing healthcare services, which is still grounded in the arts of medicine and nursing as currently taught in our institutions of higher learning. Healthcare is still very much a craft industry focused toward the one-on-one care of individual patients by clinicians, often without much consideration of long waits for patients to be seen, long process lead times, long stays in the hospital, and negative impacts on access and cost. In contrast, the shorter lead times of the team-based JIT approach allow healthcare organizations to meet the needs of patient populations while improving access, cost, and the quality and safety of care. Standardization is foundational to JIT; while still controversial among clinicians, it is an excellent starting point for the integration

---

* The term *just-in-time* has been used synonymously with TPS or Lean, but note that TPS and Lean rely on two core pillars: (1) just-in-time and (2) *jidoka* (defect prevention or mistake proofing).

of constant innovation in medicine and healthcare technologies. (Standard work is discussed in Chapter 4; for further resources, see the Appendix.)

Implementing JIT often means dramatic changes in the way processes are carried out. It will mean changed roles for clinicians and support staff and new ways of thinking about how to lay out furniture, equipment, and processes. This transformation is likely to involve a new way of scheduling based on available capacity and patient needs. It will also require teamwork and greatly enhanced attention to quality and safety. This chapter explains why these and other changes are worthwhile for you and your organization. It will also introduce you to basic JIT concepts and principles, and prepare you for learning about JIT techniques in later chapters.

3.1.1 Why JIT Is Important

Based upon a preindustrial craft model, traditional methods of healthcare are simply not capable of producing the appropriate healthcare services for large patient populations at just the right time, at just the right place, at just the right price, and in just the quantities they need. *JIT healthcare combines elements of craft and elements of modern industrial processes to help healthcare organizations become more effective—while keeping the focus on the patient—by keeping costs low, quality high, process lead times minimal, and lengths of stay clinically optimal (not too long, not too short).* It does this by eliminating waste in the process of caring for patients. It dramatically improves the quality and safety of healthcare by helping clinicians and staff to adhere to the best evidence-based practice. It also makes healthcare organizations more competitive in the rapidly changing marketplace for healthcare services.

3.1.2 The Benefits of JIT for Organizations

JIT helps a healthcare organization serve its patients better, improving access and reducing costs. JIT gives patients the services they need and providers the flexibility to serve entire populations of patients with different needs. An organization that can serve its patients this way is likely to be profitable and flexible enough to change as patient requirements, medical technology, pharmaceutical innovation, and government regulations change.

In the past, using a fee-for-service model, healthcare organizations have simply passed costs on to the patient. The pricing formula was

$$\text{Cost} + \text{Margin} = \text{Price of care}$$

As healthcare begins to move from the old fee-for-service paradigm to value-based reimbursement, healthcare organizations will receive a flat or *capitated* payment for each patient or bundle of services, regardless of the healthcare services each consumes. Meanwhile, patients and payers will insist on a competitive price. Consequently, organizations will no longer be able to pass higher costs on to patients and payers; they must reduce costs to keep their doors open. In healthcare, the new math is

$$\text{Price of care} - \text{Cost} = \text{Margin}$$

JIT healthcare methods also shorten the production lead time—the time it takes a single patient to move all the way through a process from start to finish—with excellent quality. In addition to pleasing the patient, this gives the organization an earlier return on its investment of resources to care for the patient.

What's more, *an organization that implements JIT will discover capacity that was hidden in waste.* JIT frees equipment, materials, energy, and clinicians and staff—resources that can be used to take on additional cases and care for more patients.

3.1.3 The Benefits of JIT for You

Implementing JIT also benefits you as a clinician or staff member. First, *JIT supports job security by strengthening the organization's competitiveness.* In addition, it makes the daily care of patients go smoother by

- Reducing the transport of patients, medicines, equipment, and supplies
- Improving the coordination of activities across the continuum of care
- Speeding up setups for complex procedures such as surgery
- Improving the safety of risky procedures such as drug infusion for cancer patients
- Addressing the root causes of defects and problems that cause delays
- Removing the clutter of excess materials and supplies

It is important to recognize that *learning about and participating in a JIT transformation will ultimately make you more employable* by your organization, or by any organization that hopes to stay at the top in the coming decades.

TAKE FIVE

Take a few minutes to think about these questions and to write down your answers:

- Based on what you know so far about JIT, can you see how it might benefit your patients? Would it benefit your organization? If so, how?
- Can you see how JIT might benefit you? If so, how?

3.2 PHASES OF IMPLEMENTING JIT

The implementation of JIT follows five separate phases of activity that appear in Figure 3.1.

3.2.1 Value

In the first phase of implementing JIT, it is critical to know what our patients value in terms of the timeliness, quality,

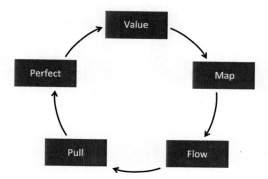

Figure 3.1 Phases of implementing JIT.

and cost of clinical care. So what is *value?* Value is defined in two ways:

1. *Value is any work performed or service provided in a timely way that the patient or his or her payers would be willing to pay for or, in other words,*
2. *Value is anything that alters (in a beneficial way) the fitness, feeling, form, or information of the patient (which the patient or payers should be willing to pay for).*

By either definition, the following items are non-value-added:

- A misdiagnosis leading to wrong treatment.
- A lab test that was not required.
- A meal that included restricted foods.
- An incorrect bill for a hospital stay.

These are all examples of non-value-added services. They contain no value, and the patient or his or her payers should be unwilling to pay for them.

Another way to understand value is to recognize what value is not *waste. Waste is any element of the healthcare process that adds cost without adding value to patient care.* Waste not only costs money; it also extends the lead time for diagnosing, prescribing, and delivering care to the patient. And it keeps the organization from doing more productive things with its resources. (See Figure 3.2.)

Time saved   Money saved   Health improved   Harm avoided

Figure 3.2   Value of JIT in healthcare.

3.2.2 Map

In the second phase of implementation, we map healthcare processes. We do this for two main reasons: first, to understand how the work is actually done and which tasks add value and which do not; and second, to envision how we might create a more reliable process in the future. The method we use to map processes is known *value stream mapping.* An example of a value stream map appears as Figure 3.3. Value stream mapping is the subject of *Mapping Clinical Value Streams* (2013), another title in the Lean Tools for Healthcare Series.

3.2.3 Flow

In the third phase of implementation, we identify where it is possible to eliminate unnecessary waits and delays in the process. When we eliminate these waits and delays, we create *flow* because patients do not wait for appointments, do not wait to be admitted, do not wait for lab results, do not

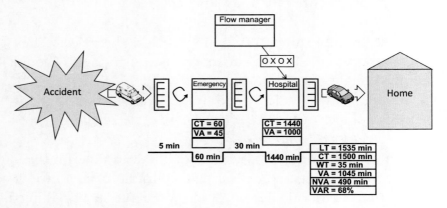

Figure 3.3   Map the continuum of care with a value stream map.

wait to be discharged, and do not wait to receive a correct bill for services rendered. Instead, they flow through the process.

The first job of JIT is to create flow wherever waits and delays can be eliminated from the process. Often, we are able to accomplish this through improvements in the assignment of clinicians and staff or in the layout of furniture, equipment, medicines, and supplies. When this is not possible because of restrictive work rules or architectural constraints, we are often able to achieve much the same result by carefully synchronizing the activities of clinicians and staff and improving their ability to communicate with one another.

In either case, the result is a newly organized and differently managed work area that we refer to as a *cell*. It is called a cell because it sometimes resembles a biological cell in its coherent function, if not its physical appearance. (Many such cells are U-shaped, like a single-celled animal with an open "mouth"; see Figure 3.4.) We will look more closely at flow in Chapter 4.

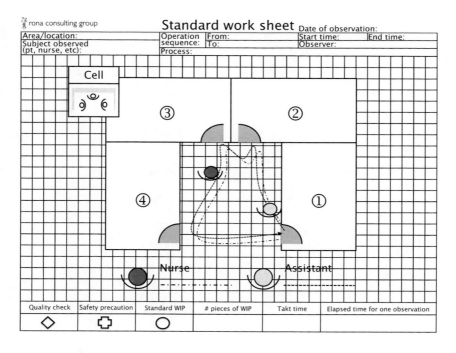

Figure 3.4 Design processes for flow, for example, by using U-shaped cells.

3.2.4 Pull

In healthcare, it is not always practical to move everything into a single cell. In these cases, the result is the creation of multiple cells or *islands of flow. The second job of JIT is to link together separate production cells—the islands of flow— through a system of patient scheduling and materials management called pull.* Pull systems regulate the waiting of patients, equipment, medicines, and supplies as they move from cell to cell so that wait times are shortened and become *predictable.* The predictability of pull stabilizes flow within individual production cells and creates a new baseline for future improvements in phase 5 of implementation.

In Figure 3.5, we see an icon for a *buffer*—a small area for patients who have been asked to wait before they can be accommodated—or pulled—by the next cell. A signal called a *kanban* is sometimes used as a means of indicating when a cell is ready to pull the next patient. We will look more closely at pull systems and kanban in Chapter 5.

3.2.5 Perfect

In the ideal JIT system, there is only pure flow; there are no buffers or pull systems because patients do not need to wait. However, JIT is always a work in progress, so we build in adaptability during the fifth phase of implementation, known as *perfect.* To perfect a Lean process, we employ the Plan–Do–Check–Act (PDCA) process of total quality management

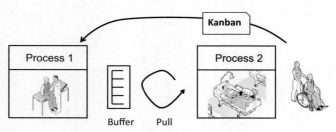

The patient is "pulled" by the next downstream process, but only when it is ready to serve the patient. When Process 2 discharges a patient, a kanban card is sent to Process 1.

Figure 3.5 Pull the care process with buffers and kanban.

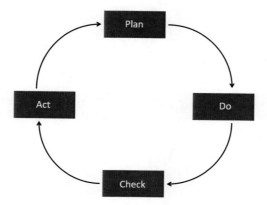

Figure 3.6 Perfect the process with PDCA cycles.

to identify where we may eliminate remaining process delays and other process wastes including, of course, defects. (See Figure 3.6.)

TAKE FIVE

Take a few minutes to think about these questions and to write down your answers:

- What wastes can you see in your process? Which do you think are the most serious problems at your organization?
- What problems does waiting cause in your hospital, clinic, or lab?
- What problems arise when clinicians and staff members hide errors and accidents that occur in your hospital, clinic, or lab?

SUMMARY

Just-in-time (often called JIT for short) is an approach that enables a healthcare organization to efficiently and reliably produce the quality services its patients require—when they need them, where they need them, and in the amount they need. Implementing JIT often means changes in the way processes are carried out, in the roles of clinicians and support staff; in the layout of furniture, equipment, and processes; and in how scheduling is done.

JIT healthcare combines elements of craft and elements of modern industrial processes to help healthcare organizations become more effective—while keeping the focus on the patient—by keeping costs low, quality high, process lead times minimal, and lengths of stay clinically optimal (not too long, not too short). It does this by eliminating waste in the process of caring for patients.

JIT helps a healthcare organization serve its patients better, improving access and reducing costs. In the past, healthcare organizations passed costs on to the patient or payer:

$$\text{Cost} + \text{Profit} = \text{Price of care}$$

Today, patients and payers insist on a competitive price, so organizations must reduce costs to make profits:

$$\text{Price of care} - \text{Cost} = \text{Profit}$$

JIT healthcare methods also shorten the production lead time, freeing wasted capacity in equipment, materials, energy, and clinician and staff time.

JIT benefits clinicians and staff members by strengthening the organization's competitiveness, which supports job security. It also makes the daily care of patients go smoother by eliminating various wastes that cause problems.

The implementation of JIT follows five phases:

1. *Value.* Define value, and waste, in the eyes of the patient and payers. Waste is any element of the healthcare process that adds cost without adding value to patient care.
2. *Map.* Use value stream mapping to understand how the work is done and which tasks add value, and to create more reliable processes in the future.
3. *Flow.* Eliminate waits and delays in the process of patient care, by rearranging the layout of processes into cells, or by synchronizing the activities of clinicians and staff.

4. *Pull.* Connect cells, or islands of flow, by regulating the waiting of patients, equipment, medicines, and supplies as they move from cell to cell so that wait times are shortened and become predictable.
5. *Perfect.* Employ the PDCA cycle to eliminate remaining process delays and wastes, including defects.

REFLECTIONS

Now that you have completed this chapter, take a few minutes to think about these questions and to write down your answers:

- What did you learn from reading this chapter that stands out as particularly useful or interesting?
- Do you have any questions about the topics presented in this chapter? If so, what are they?
- What additional information do you need to fully understand the ideas presented in this chapter?

Chapter 4

Creating Islands of Flow

4.1 INTRODUCTION

To achieve flow in healthcare so that patients receive just the care they need, just-in-time (JIT), we must first create standard work. Standard work stabilizes operations, increases reliability, and begins to make processes predictable. See *Standard Work for Lean Healthcare* (2011). Once we have implemented standard work, we can establish flow, which refines standard work and synchronizes the activities of clinicians and staff with the actual demand for healthcare services. This results in the creation of healthcare production units, called *cells*, in which patients experience very few waits or delays.

4.2 STANDARD WORK

Standard processes are the foundation for high-quality, safe, JIT care for patients and JIT delivery of medicines, test information, meals, and supplies. In a Lean healthcare system, later or *downstream* processes count on the ability of earlier or *upstream* processes to care for patients within a more or less certain time frame, called *cycle time*. If the cycle time of the upstream process is unpredictable, JIT delivery to the downstream process can't happen, often leading to poor quality and high risk to patient safety. When healthcare processes are not predictable, patients wait for clinicians, and clinicians wait for patients; patient satisfaction declines; and healthcare costs rise. So, as you begin to improve your processes and the operations within them, you must standardize the way the work is done at every step.

Most clinical processes contain so much waste that JIT cannot function until standards are set and improvements are made. Poor standardization of workflows gives rise to three types of waste:

1. *Overproduction:* When processes are poorly standardized as to cycle time, they do not easily permit precise scheduling. Managers often compensate by *overproducing*, that is, by working ahead of the stated schedule or providing services *just-in-case* instead of *just-in-time*. When coupled with the misaligned incentives of fee for service, this can lead to the overproduction of services for patients who did not require them.

2. *Overprocessing:* Poorly standardized processes often include more than the necessary number of steps or unnecessary repetition of steps. Such processes are said to *overprocess* patients or process inputs such as medicines, supplies, and information. Overprocessing frequently occurs where process reliability is low and clinicians and staff mistrust the process.

3. *Defects:* Poorly standardized processes often lead to inadvertent clinical defects, some of which can result in injury or death.

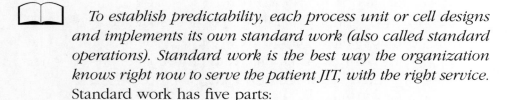

To establish predictability, each process unit or cell designs and implements its own standard work (also called standard operations). Standard work is the best way the organization knows right now to serve the patient JIT, with the right service. Standard work has five parts:

1. Standard task
2. Standard work sequence
3. Standard cycle time
4. Standard patients in process
5. Standard documentation

4.2.1 Standard Task

In every industry, including the healthcare industry, each process must be broken down into individual work tasks. Tasks are the basic steps or building blocks of operations and processes. In order to make processes predictable, each task in every work sequence must first be standardized. Otherwise, the work content of the process may vary significantly from clinician to clinician or from staff member to staff member. *Documenting each task carried out by clinicians and staff helps ensure that each task is performed in the same way—the best way we know now—each time.*

4.2.2 Standard Work Sequence

It is impossible to achieve predictability without a consistent work sequence. Without a standard sequence, the order in which tasks are performed may vary even when the tasks are standardized. So the sequence of tasks, as well as the tasks themselves, must be standardized. *Documenting the sequence of tasks ensures that tasks are performed in the same order—the best order we know now—each time.*

4.2.3 Standard Cycle Time

Standardizing task and sequence is not enough because it is impossible to have a predictable process, unless the *time* it takes to complete the process is also standardized. *Cycle time is the actual, observed time required to complete a process.* Cycle time is determined by timing the operations in a process from start to finish, including manual work, walking, waiting, and inspection, and adding any time required for information systems or machines to do their value-added work. (See Figure 4.1.) Operations are usually clocked several times; the most frequently recurring time (or *mode*) is used as the current standard cycle time.

   Process cycle time determines whether a process is capable of producing the quantity required by the next process at

31

rona consulting group   **Time Observation Form**

Area/location: **Emergency department**	Date of observation: **December 31**
Subject observed: **Patient**	Start time: **11:30 pm**
Process: **Door to doc**	Observer: **Nancy**

Step no.	Description of operation	Observation time Observations 1	2	3	4	5	Mode (most occurring) freq. task time	Remarks
1	*Greet*	0 / 3:30	0:00 / 3:00	0:00 / 4:00	—	—	3:30	
2	*Wait*	3:30 / 5:00	3:00 / 5:30	4:00 / 2:00	—	—	5:00	
3	*Triage*	8:30 / 7:00	8:30 / 8:30	6:00 / 3:00	—	—	7:00	3rd patient had chest pain
4	*Wait*	15:30 / 5:00	17:30 / 4:00	9:00 / 1:00	—	—	4:00	
5		20:30	21:00	10:0...				

Figure 4.1 Time observation form.

the required time. The time requirements of each process are ultimately controlled by the takt time for the value stream. *Takt* is a German word that means *beat*; *takt time* refers to the rate at which a process must be completed in order to meet demand, and it is stated in terms of time per patient (see Takt Time box).

For example, the discharge rate required by a hospital to facilitate admitting all new patients who need to be seen is the hospital's takt time. If a process does not discharge patients as fast as needed, an *inventory* of patients waiting to be admitted will accumulate. This is because, on average, the number of admits must equal the number of discharges (or deaths). Worse, patients waiting to be admitted may leave without being seen or may be diverted to other facilities. A production backlog or physical buildup of patients in waiting rooms is an indicator of insufficient capacity and should lead to process improvement.

4.2.4 Standard Patients in Process

To standardize the work that takes place in a process, you must also standardize the minimum number of patients and the quantity of medicines and supplies needed to complete

one processing cycle and allow the cycle to continue. *The goal is to aim for the smooth flow of patients, medicines, and supplies through the process.* This means that individual patients and the medicines and supplies they need move directly from one operation to the next rather than piling up between operations. Standardizing patients in process or other work in process further stabilizes the process cycle time; if work in process is allowed to vary, the process cycle time will also vary.

TAKT TIME

Takt time is the rate of patient or customer demand, and the rate at which work needs to be completed to meet that demand. It is calculated by dividing the average demand (e.g., number of patients to be seen) into the time available for providing services:

Takt time = Available time/Average demand

For example, if an urgent care clinic is open from 8 a.m. to 8 p.m., with all meals and breaks staggered to provide continuous care, the available time is 12 hours, or 720 minutes. If, on average, 60 patients present themselves for care each day, the takt time, or the rate of demand, is calculated as follows:

Available time/Average demand =
720 minutes/60 patients = 12-minute takt time

Note that this does not mean that each patient encounter takes 12 minutes. It is the rate that, on average, patients will need to move from one process to the next, and the rate at which, on average, we should see patients leaving at the end of the last process.

4.2.5 Standard Documentation

Organizations document their standard work on a set of standard forms. (See Figure 4.2.) They may use different names

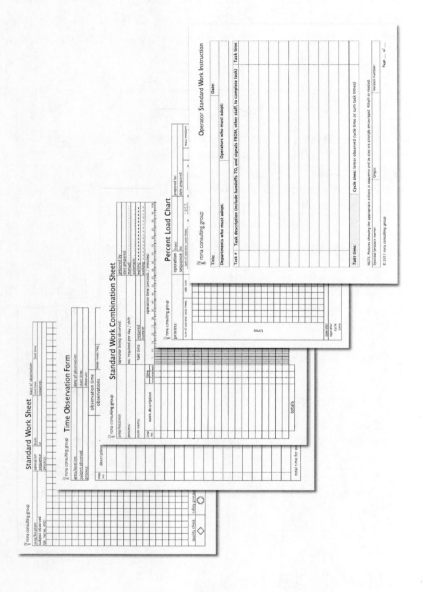

Figure 4.2 Standard work documentation.

for these forms or combine them in different ways, but the functions are similar. Commonly used forms include the following:

- *Time observation form* (see Figure 4.1): This form documents the tasks, sequence of tasks, task times, and cycle time for each unique operation (or sequence of tasks) performed by an individual clinician or staff member.
- *Standard work sheet* (see Figure 4.3): This form documents the current standard sequence of processing steps and the equipment layout for this sequence.
- *Standard work combination sheet* (see Figure 4.4): This form charts the relationship between machine operation time and human work time in a process.
- *Percent load chart* (see Figures 4.9 and 4.10): This form documents the capability of all clinicians and staff members working together in a process to meet takt time.

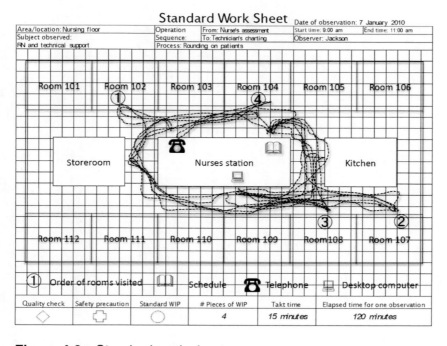

Figure 4.3 Standard work sheet.

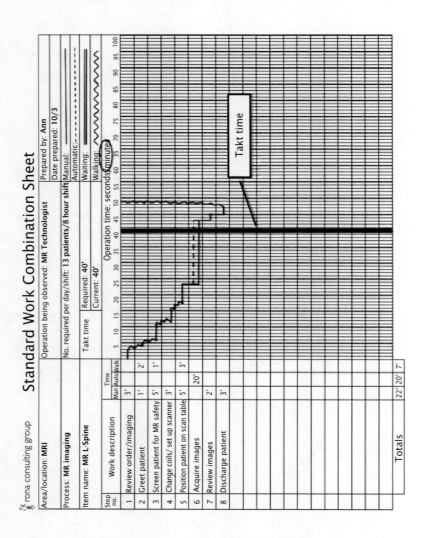

rona consulting group — Standard Work Combination Sheet

Area/location: **MRI**	Operation being observed: **MR Technologist**
	Prepared by: **Ann**
	Date prepared: **10/3**
Process: **MR imaging**	No. required per day/shift: **13 patients/8 hour shift**
Item name: **MR L-Spine**	Takt time — Required: **40'** / Current: **40'**

Legend: Manual: —— / Automatic: - - - / Waiting: ══ / Walking: ∿∿∿

Step no.	Work description	Time Man	Time Auto	Time Walk
1	Review order/imaging	3'		
2	Greet patient	1'		2'
3	Screen patient for MR safety	5'		1'
4	Change coils/ set up scanner	3'		
5	Position patient on scan table	5'		3'
6	Acquire images		20'	
7	Review images	2'		
8	Discharge patient	3'		
	Totals	22'	20'	7'

Operation time: seconds/minutes — scale 5 10 15 20 25 30 35 40 45 50 55 60 65 70 75 80 85 90 95 100

Takt time

Figure 4.4 Standard work combination sheet.

TAKE FIVE

Take a few minutes to think about these questions and to write down your answers:

- Do you know the cycle time for the processes in your work area?
- Is work done using a consistent sequence and method?
- How much work in process is in your work area at any given time?

4.2.6 The Foundation for Continuous Improvement

Of course, standard work is the best way we know how to perform a sequence of tasks *today*. What about tomorrow? What happens when we discover a new and better way to care for patients? Developing standard work is only the beginning. *Standardization is the first step in improvement.* (See Figure 4.5.) Standard work defines the method used by everyone—but it is also a *living* standard that should be continuously improving.

Standard work helps to bring processes under control and thus to make them predictable. This must be the case to support the JIT synchronization of healthcare services from one healthcare process to another. When clinical defects arise,

Figure 4.5 Standards as the baseline for improvement.

STANDARD WORK VERSUS
THE ART OF MEDICINE

Some clinicians object to standard work because it seems to compromise the *art of medicine*, that is, the special discretion that clinicians are taught to exercise when diagnosing patients and prescribing treatments. With the advent of evidence-based medicine, the scope of this art is slowly being circumscribed by a growing body of evidence that supports the adoption of relatively standardized diagnostic tests and treatments. In addition, the shift from fee-for-service to value-based healthcare asks clinicians to consider the needs of populations, as well as the needs of individual patients, which also supports standardized diagnoses and treatments in some cases. For the time being, however, much of medicine—and nursing, for that matter—is art. Doctors, nurses, and other clinicians *should* vary their care based on the individual differences of their patients. Improving and standardizing process flows improves predictability and quality conditions, and supports clinicians' abilities to practice their art. Flows that lend themselves to standardization and to JIT include:

- The physical flow of patients through outpatient clinics
- The physical flow of samples of tissue and fluids from patients through the lab
- The physical flow of patients through imaging departments
- The physical flow of patients through the emergency department
- The physical flow of patients through surgery
- The physical flow of patients through the hospital
- The physical flow of meals through hospital kitchens to patient rooms

All of these flows, including many of the nonmedical steps within them, can be standardized without compromising or even touching the arts of medicine or nursing. Indeed, by reducing the variation in practice and in cycle time that currently exist in these processes, more time can be made for physicians and nurses to practice their craft under greatly improved conditions. In fact, the vast majority of medical errors in U.S. hospitals are not failures of individual clinicians; they occur in the handoffs between processes and between clinicians. These handoffs can all be standardized and improved without compromising the art of medicine.

the standardization of task and sequence is also a necessary condition of root cause analysis. Without such standardization, there is no stable baseline from which to measure process defects, which are naturally defined as deviations from standard practice. Without the standardization of task and sequence, it is difficult or impossible to determine what happened in the first place, let alone how it went wrong. Standardization helps the people in the workplace understand when the process is out of standard or *out of control* and sets the stage for improvement. Only by doing work the same way each time can you know whether trial changes are having the desired result.

TAKE FIVE

Take a few minutes to think about these questions and to write down your answers:

- How are standards for processes and operations currently developed in your workplace?
- Do your clinicians object to standard work because it limits their discretion? If so, what are some objections you've heard, and how might you respond to them?
- What processes in your workplace might be standardized without compromising the arts of medicine or nursing?

4.3 BENEFITS OF A PROCESS FLOW LAYOUT

Poor process layout is another symptom of poor standardization, and it gives rise to its own set of problems. Many organizations group their clinicians, support staff, furniture, and equipment according to the types of healthcare operation performed.

For example, lab equipment is physically located in the lab department. Radiology equipment is located in the radiology department. Registration activities occur in a special registration area. (See Figure 4.6.)

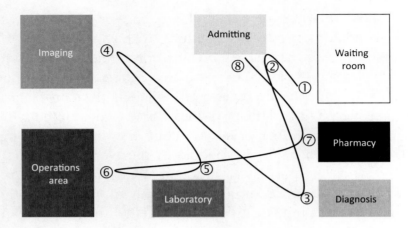

Figure 4.6   Operations-based layout.

   This operations-based layout leads to four additional types of waste associated with poor standardization:

1. *Transportation:* Most processes include operations in several different physical areas and/or on several different types of equipment. To reach the next step in the process, medicines, equipment, and supplies must often travel to another area. This travel requires personnel (transporters) and equipment (wheelchairs, mobile beds, carts, dollies), but it adds no value to the care of the patient.
2. *Motion:* For the same reason that poorly laid out processes create unnecessary transportation, they give rise to the waste of motion as clinicians and staff must often walk from one area to another to complete their work cycles. Like transportation, motion adds no value to patient care.
3. *Inventory:* Operations-based layouts tend to generate inventories of medicines waiting to be dispensed and supplies waiting to be transported significant distances from one area to another.
4. *Waiting:* Operations-based layouts tend to generate patients waiting to be seen by the next clinician or staff member who must move significant distances from one patient to another.

Assigning multiple personnel to the same or contingent areas, with furniture, equipment, medicines, and supplies positioned closely together in the order of the processing tasks, reduces waste and improves the flow in several ways. For one thing, *placing personnel and equipment for each task side by side eliminates much of the waste of transporting patients, equipment, medicines, and supplies long distances* (see Figure 4.7). This is sometimes referred to as a *process-based layout* and is also known as a *production line.*

What's more, *a process-based layout allows patients to flow through the process without waiting between steps.* This approach, called *flow processing,* eliminates delays and saves space so that equipment, medicines, supplies, *and patients flow through the process quicker. A process-based layout also improves handoffs between clinicians and staff members.* This all helps to reduce the cost of healthcare and make it more accessible, affordable, and safe.

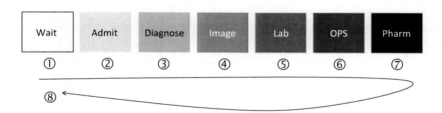

Figure 4.7 Process-based layout.

TAKE FIVE

Take a few minutes to think about these questions and to write down your answers:

- How are personnel, furniture, and equipment arranged in your workplace?
- Do you think this layout has waste in it? If so, what kinds?
- What other types of waste can you identify that are connected to poor process standardization?

4.3.1 U-Shaped Cells

As automaker Henry Ford demonstrated over a century ago, it is possible to implement flow processing by arranging the personnel, furniture, and equipment for each operation in a straight line, as shown in Figure 4.7. However, when the patient, clinician, or staff member finishes the last step of the process, he or she must walk back to the first step to leave the area (in the case of the patient) or to start again (in the case of the clinician or staff member). This walking is waste that adds no value to the care of the patient.

To eliminate this waste, flow processing often uses an arrangement called a *U-shaped cell. A cell is a well-integrated process consisting of coordinated, standardized sequences of standardized tasks. These tasks may be performed by one or more clinicians and/or staff members. Furthermore, the cell is normally capable of meeting its takt time.* (See Figure 4.8.) In a U-shaped cell, patients, personnel, furniture, and equipment are placed in process sequence in a horseshoe pattern. In this layout, *the last processing step is very close to the first step, so patients, clinicians, and staff are not walking as far to leave the area or begin the next cycle.* Within each cell, each clinician and staff member performs standard work that is

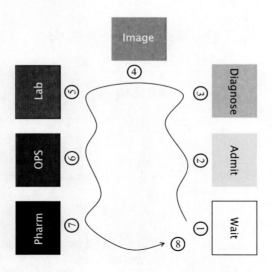

Figure 4.8 U-shaped cell.

synchronized with the work of every other team member. The work of all team members is synchronized with takt time or the rate of patient demand.

TAKE FIVE

Take a few minutes to think about these questions and to write down your answers:

- How does a U-shaped layout eliminate waste in health-care processes?
- Do you think the equipment in your area is better suited to caring for patients in an operations-based layout or to caring for patients one at a time in a process-based layout, or flow? Why?

4.3.2 Team-Based Operations

Within each U-shaped cell, clinicians and staff members must operate as a team by carefully synchronizing their activities. It is not enough to hold pep talks and state how much we value each other as team members. Clinicians must learn to practice like a high-performance sports team, in which each team member knows exactly where every other team member is on the playing field. Also, the coordination of timing must be perfect. In order for process cycle times to be predictable, the cycle time of each clinician and staff member in the process must also be predictable and capable of meeting the needs of each patient. If the cycle times of clinicians or staff are unpredictable or too long, or team members cannot synchronize their activities, the team will fail to coordinate their activities to meet demand. In addition, defects may creep into the process. As cycle times and defects grow, costs rise and patient satisfaction declines.

 To ensure that each clinician and staff member within a cell has a predictable cycle time that meets patient needs, we analyze the cell with a *percent load chart*. (See Figures 4.9 and 4.10.) This chart shows how each clinician or staff member is

43

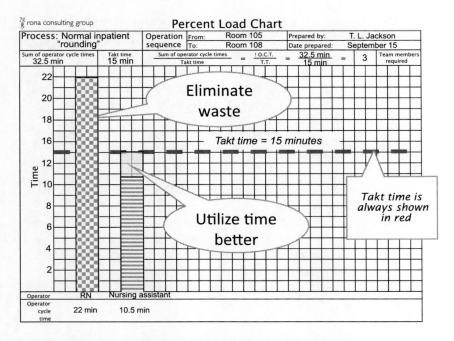

Figure 4.9   Percent load chart, before improvement.

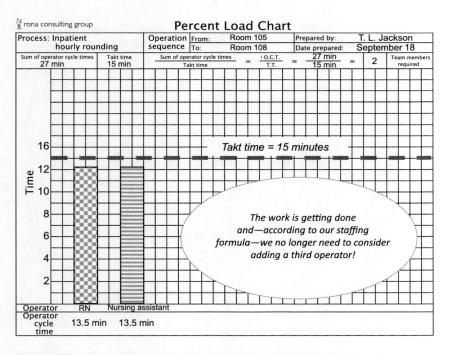

Figure 4.10   Percent load chart, after improvement.

loaded with work within the cell by recording the observed cycle time of each care team member in a separate bar. The bars are drawn relative to takt time, the time by which each operator must complete an entire work process in order to meet the expected demand for our team's services. Takt time is illustrated as a horizontal line, which is always drawn in red. If the bar for a given clinician or staff member rises above the red takt time line, we know immediately that we must help that person improve their standard work. In Figure 4.9, we can easily see that the registered nurse (RN; represented by the bar on the left) is loaded with work and cannot meet takt time. In Figure 4.10, we see that the work has been redistributed and improved, so now both the RN and the nursing assistant can meet takt time, without the need to consider adding another staff member to the process.

To ensure that each clinician and staff member within a cell knows how to synchronize his or her activities with other members on the team, we build a *swim lane diagram*. (See Figure 4.11.) *A swim lane diagram shows exactly what work is being performed by each team member at each moment from the beginning of the process to the end.* Some teams embed communication devices, like pagers, cell phones, or simple cards or flags (called *kanban*) in the

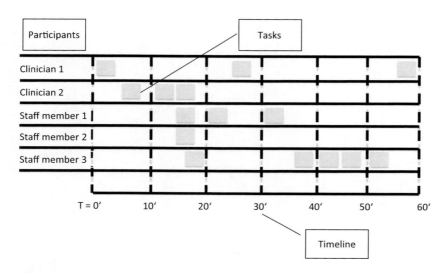

Figure 4.11 Swim lane diagram.

45

workplace to ensure that everyone, including patients, can keep track of where they are in the process.

Even though existing architecture, government regulations, or professional practice limitations may restrict your ability to move patients, personnel, and equipment physically closer together, you can still create cells for healthcare that meet takt time through team-based operations supported by percent load charts and swim lane diagrams.

4.3.3 Stopping to Fix Defects

In order for healthcare cells to function properly—predictably, and with reliable quality and safety—not only must clinicians and staff meet takt time; they must also stop to fix defects as they occur or as they are discovered.

In healthcare, the only technology required for stopping to fix defects in handoffs is a simple checklist. Checklists, or *checks* for short, are used at critical points in the process, where defects normally tend to occur or where quality must be perfect. Checks come in two basic varieties:

1. *Successive checks:* Successive checks are checks made by a clinician or staff member *before* their work cycle begins. These checks ensure that all required information is received and that work completed previously by other clinicians or staff has been done correctly, ensuring clinical quality and patient safety. (See Figure 4.12.)

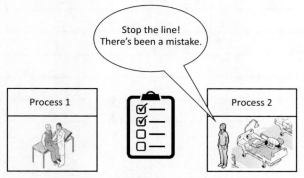

Stop the line before work begins.

Figure 4.12   Successive checks.

JUST-IN-TIME REQUIRES *JUST CULTURE*

In 2012, the Department of Health and Human Services found that only one in seven adverse events, or defects, is reported.* There are many reasons why an event might not be reported, including staff misperceptions about what requires reporting. For JIT to work, successive checks, self-checks, and mistake proofing must result in reporting as many defects as are made. For this to occur, everyone must be educated about what needs to be reported. But it must also be safe for clinicians and staff to say, "I made a defect" or "I discovered a defect," and say so as soon as possible. It is recognized that the culture of healthcare today may not always be a just culture—a culture of trust, learning, and accountability—rather than a culture that is focused only on punishing those who make (or report) errors.

---

* Department of Health and Human Services, Office of Inspector General. 2012. *Hospital Incident Reporting Systems Do Not Capture Most Patient Harm.* OEI-06-09-00091, January.

2. *Self-checks:* Self-checks are checks by made a clinician or staff member *after* his or her own work cycle has been completed. Self-checks ensure that each clinician has completed his or her tasks correctly and in the right sequence—and that the patient is safe—before handing the patient off to the next clinician or staff member in the process. (See Figure 4.13.)

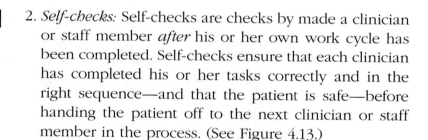

Stop the line before work is complete.

Figure 4.13 Self-checks.

In Chapter 6, we will examine a third type of checklist used to mistake-proof processes.

4.3.4 Improved Handoffs

Because the distances between clinicians and staff are often reduced within a U-shaped cell, the wait times for patients are also reduced, and the handoffs from one clinician or staff member to another are made in real time. Some handoffs can be eliminated from the process entirely. This has the effect of increasing process quality. Communication is one of the most frequently named root causes contributing to sentinel events.* Communication errors often occur during patient handoffs. Therefore, it is essential to ensure that information passed during handoffs is error-free and unambiguous. Coupled with the Lean or JIT practice of stopping to fix defects as they occur, real-time handoffs within U-shaped cells go a long way to addressing one of the most important problems in healthcare today.

TAKE FIVE

Take a few minutes to think about these questions and to write down your answers:

- Do people in your work area use checklists for successive checks or self-checks?
- If so, what are some of the things they check for?
- Can you think of some specific areas where successive checks or self-checks might help you in your processes?

SUMMARY

Standard processes are the foundation for high-quality, safe, JIT care for patients and JIT delivery of medicines, test information,

---

* Joint Commission. Sentinel event data: Root causes by event type, 2004–2Q 2014. Available at http://www.jointcommission.org/Sentinel_Event_Statistics/ (accessed February 19, 2015).

meals, and supplies. To establish predictability, each process unit or cell designs and implements its own standard work (also called standard operations). Standard work is the best way the organization knows right now to serve the patient JIT, with the right service. Standard work has five components:

1. Standard task
2. Standard work sequence
3. Standard cycle time
4. Standard patients in process
5. Standard documentation

Organizations document their standard operations on a set of forms:

- Time observation form
- Standard work sheet
- Standard work combination sheet
- Percent load chart

Standard work is developed by the people who do the work. Standardization helps people in the workplace understand when the process is out of standard and sets the stage for improvement. Standard work is a *living* standard that should be continuously improving.

Most clinical processes contain so much waste that JIT cannot work until standards are set and improvements are made. Process improvements to eliminate waste often include changes in the array of personnel, furniture, equipment, and supplies in the outpatient clinic, hospital, and lab.

Positioning personnel, furniture, and equipment closely together in the order of the processing steps reduces waste and improves the flow. Placing the personnel and equipment for each step side by side eliminates much of the waste of transporting patients, medicines, and supplies long distances. A process-based layout also allows patients and supplies to flow through the process without long waits between steps, and it improves handoffs between clinicians and staff members.

Flow processing often uses an arrangement called a U-shaped cell, in which the patients, personnel, furniture, and equipment are placed in process sequence in a horseshoe pattern. In this layout, the last step is very close to the first step, so the operator does not have to walk far to begin the next cycle of care. Within each U-shaped cell, clinicians and staff members must operate as a team by carefully synchronizing their activities, with predictable cycle times. They also stop to fix defects as they occur, using successive checks and self-checks to help mistake-proof processes.

REFLECTIONS

Now that you have completed this chapter, take a few minutes to think about these questions and to write down your answers:

- What did you learn from reading this chapter that stands out as particularly useful or interesting?
- Do you have any questions about the topics presented in this chapter? If so, what are they?
- What additional information do you need to fully understand the ideas presented in this chapter?

Chapter 5

Using Pull to Connect Islands of Flow

5.1 INTRODUCTION

Chapter 4 described how to eliminate waiting and improve quality with the introduction of islands of flow. These islands are created by reorganizing clinicians and staff members in U-shaped cells that minimize transportation and motion and improve communication and handoffs. This chapter describes how just-in-time teams and U-shaped cells are connected in a system using *pull.*

Pull is a method for creating a system of production in which a downstream process producing to takt time signals to an upstream process that it is ready for the next patient, product, or other unit of work. Pull systems control the production of healthcare services. They also control the movement and wait times of patients, or other work, between processes that cannot be combined into a production cell. Therefore, pull is an approach to scheduling that preserves the synchronicity of teamwork and the predictability of flow. Bear in mind that this is a general overview and that organizations may implement these concepts in different ways. (See Figure 5.1.) For more information about these concepts, see the resources listed in the Appendix.

5.2 KANBAN AND PULL SYSTEMS

In a just-in-time system of production cells, the movement of patients, clinicians, medicines, and supplies is coordinated across the continuum of care—from cell to cell or, in other words, from one island of flow to another.

Figure 5.1 Basic concepts of just-in-time and pull production.

This coordination is critical in avoiding delays and preserving the synchronicity and predictability of services. To achieve this coordination, organizations use a device called *kanban. The word kanban means "signal card" but can refer generally to any type of signal.* With kanban, cards or other visual or electronic signals control the movement of patients, medicines, and supplies (see Figure 5.2) and synchronize that movement with takt time, the pace of production inside the cells.

Kanban is a mechanism for transforming the continuum of care into a *pull production system. In a pull system, a clinical cell or process (Process A) sees its next patient only when the succeeding cell or process (Process B) is ready to see the patient who has just been seen by Process A. Likewise, medicines and supplies are moved from one process to another only when the next process signals that it needs more.* When kanban are used to connect two cells or processes, the processes are linked almost mechanically, like gears in a Swiss-made watch. In effect, patients, medicines, and supplies from the earlier process are *pulled* when the next process indicates with a kanban that it is ready for them.

| Card | Flag | Empty chair | Text/ email | EHR | Light | Sound |

Figure 5.2 A kanban system can use many kinds of signals.

In a series of processes, the pull normally begins with the production schedule for the rate-limiting (that is, the longest) process. The schedule for that process is based on actual or expected demand. Examples of rate-limiting processes might include the following:

- Meeting with the physician or nurse practitioner in a primary care clinic
- The discharge process in a hospital
- The surgery process in the perioperative theater

The rate-limiting process is often called the pacemaker. The pacemaker process uses kanban to pull needed patients, medicines, and supplies from the previous process, which pulls from the process before it, and so on. (See Figure 5.3.)

Using a pacemaker to establish the rhythm of service production prevents confusion about which patients to see next, which tests to run, which prescriptions to prepare, which meals to cook, and so on. In contrast, *the more traditional "push" production systems often used in healthcare depend on seeing patients, performing tests, and moving medicines and supplies according to separate, predetermined schedules.* Often, these processes and their schedules are not linked together in a predictable or smooth way. Production priorities can easily become confused. When this happens, prior processes will continue to push patients, tests, medicines, and supplies forward even when the next processes are not ready for them. As a result, patients may wait to be seen by the next process. When the push approach is applied to the movement of medicines and

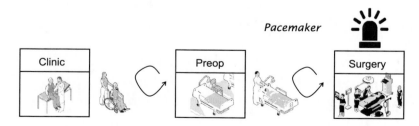

Figure 5.3 Setting the pace. Starting with the pacemaker (in this case, surgery), the downstream process pulls the patient from the next upstream process, but only when it is ready to serve the patient.

supplies, excess inventories pile up on shelves. Push can also force downstream processes to wait. Doctors wait for patients, while medicines and supplies are stocked out.

5.3 BENEFITS OF A PULL SYSTEM

 The main benefit of pull systems is that they are very responsive to actual changes in demand. Push systems rely almost entirely upon forecasts of demand. They tend to be unresponsive to changes in demand that occur once production has begun. In contrast, pull systems take forecasts as a starting point and then build in flexibility so that the movement of patients, medicines, and supplies can be adjusted in real time, based upon changes in actual demand throughout the day.

Additional benefits of pull systems include the following:

- Backlogs of patients waiting for appointments can be identified and cleared.
- Time can be set aside in the schedule to see patients who need urgent care.
- Time can be set aside in the schedule to accommodate same-day appointments.
- Inventories of expensive medicines and supplies can be cut in half.
- The space required to house waiting patients and excess inventories can be devoted to more valuable purposes.

5.4 TYPES OF KANBAN IN A PULL SYSTEM

A typical pull system uses four main types of kanban cards or devices (see Figure 5.4):

 1. *Production kanban:* Authorizes the previous process to see more patients.
2. *Rooming or restock kanban:* Authorizes a process to transfer patients, medicines, or supplies from the previous process.

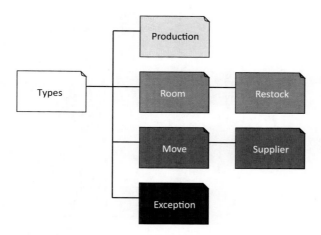

Figure 5.4 The four main types of kanban.

3. *Move or supplier kanban:* Authorizes an outside supplier to deliver more medicines and supplies.
4. *Exception kanban:* Authorizes production, restocking,
or movement in special recurring cases that may be
difficult to anticipate.

Sections 5.4.1 through 5.4.4 give simple explanations of how
the four types of kanban are used to control production.

5.4.1 Production Kanban

In a clinical setting, a production kanban signals the delivery
of clinical services, such as discharge from a hospital. In
Figure 5.5, a transporter is dispatched by the scheduler to
take Patient 1 to his car. She carries a kanban that signals the
final preparation of Patient 2 for discharge. While the transporter removes Patient 1 from the hospital floor, the production kanban carried by the transporter acts as a signal to the
nurses on the hospital floor to prepare Patient 2 for discharge.
In effect, the discharge kanban pulls Patient 2 from his or her
room into the final phases of the discharge process. A rooming kanban then triggers the admission to the hospital of
Patient 3.

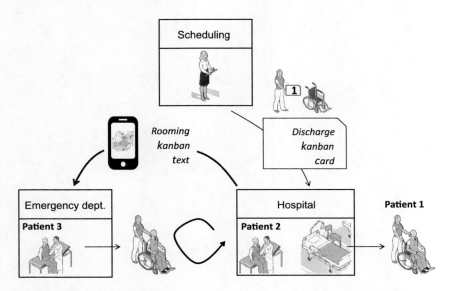

Figure 5.5 Pull the care process with kanban. The patient is pulled by the next downstream process. In this picture, scheduling sends a production or discharge kanban card with a transporter to the hospital floor. Patient 1 is discharged and goes home, while Patient 2 is prepared for discharge. Meanwhile, a rooming kanban text message is sent to the emergency department to admit Patient 3.

Production kanban can also be used to manage production processes in which healthcare creates a physical product, such as the following:

- Medical tests
- Drug prescriptions
- Hot meals
- Equipment maintenance

5.4.2 Rooming or *Restock* Kanban

Rooming kanban are used to move patients from one cell to another. In Figure 5.5, there are two cells: (1) the hospital itself and (2) the emergency room. When the hospital bed in which Patient 1 was staying is vacated, a rooming kanban is sent to the emergency room, to signal that Patient 3 should be admitted from emergency to the hospital. Patient 3 will occupy the bed vacated by Patient 1, which will be cleaned and resupplied before Patient 3 arrives. According to the rules of kanban (see Section 5.5), the emergency room will not send another patient to the floor until it receives a kanban or signal from the hospital that it is ready to admit.

When kanban are applied to the movement of medicines and supplies, each cell in the care continuum or value stream will normally have an inbound storage area. In the storage area are containers that hold a small, fixed quantity of medicines or supplies used in the cell. Each container in the storage area has a move kanban attached to it. When the cell begins to process the contents of a container, the restock kanban is taken off the container and brought to a central storeroom or warehouse. The kanban acts as a signal to materials management to replenish the medicines or supplies actually consumed by the cell that returned the kanban. The restock kanban is attached to a new, full container, which is taken back to the inbound stock area of the cell, ready for use.

5.4.3 Move or Supplier Kanban

For medicines and supplies that are made by outside suppliers rather than by in-house processes, a move or supplier kanban is used in place of a restock kanban. Move kanban are attached by suppliers to full containers, which travel from the supplier to the in-house inbound area. When the in-house cells begin to consume the medicines or supplies in that container, the move kanban is removed and sent to the outside supplier as a signal to replenish the depleted supplies.

TAKE FIVE

Take a few minutes to think about these questions and to write down your answers:

- Do you think your organization currently uses a push system or a pull system?
- What issues do you see with the way service production or the replenishment of medicines and supplies is scheduled at your facility?

5.4.4 Exception Kanban

 In healthcare, patients are frequently not stable, which means that their respective conditions may change unexpectedly, requiring new diagnoses and new treatments. Depending upon the acuity or seriousness of their conditions, which can be measured, we are frequently able to predict how often this may happen and what the likely outcomes may be, even if we cannot know exactly when it will happen. Exception kanban can be used to accommodate rapid response to patients who need immediate attention, while preserving the synchronicity and predictability in a pull system.

5.5 BASIC RULES OF KANBAN

Five basic rules must be followed for successful use of kanban:

1. Downstream processes signal to upstream processes when they are ready for the next patient.
2. Upstream processes do not send patients to downstream processes until they receive a kanban or signal; they begin to care for the next patient *only once they have sent the last patient downstream*.
3. All processes produce and deliver only 100% defect-free services to their patients or customers.
4. Production is leveled across all processes, in order to synchronize it and prevent overproduction and waiting.
5. The kanban that govern the production of services for a patient tend to travel with the patient.

5.6 BUFFERS AND SUPERMARKETS

In Chapter 4, we described how patients flow through process-based operations or U-shaped cells without waiting to be seen. Ideally, all healthcare services would be organized into one, giant U-shaped cell in which patients never wait for clinicians and clinicians never wait for patients. For many reasons, this is not often possible, and so we create islands of flow that we then link with pull systems and kanban.

In between these cells or islands, patients will wait to be seen. Sometimes, they wait because they must walk or be transported long distances to another department or building— even to another city. Sometimes, they wait because there is an exceptionally high demand for the next process in the continuum of care. Whatever the reason for the wait, *pull systems make the wait shorter and predictable.*

Pull systems employ two different mechanisms to ensure that wait times between production cells are short and predictable. The first mechanism is known as a *FIFO lane.* The second mechanism is known as a *buffer.*

5.6.1 FIFO Lanes

FIFO means "first-in, first-out." FIFO lanes are small waiting areas where patients wait to be seen in the same order in which they first entered the FIFO lane. FIFO lanes are appropriate for most scheduled services or anywhere patients are in stable condition and where their pain is under control. No one needs to *get out of line.* (See Figure 5.6a.)

The maximum number of patients in a FIFO lane between two processes is determined by the travel time between the processes and the production pace or demand of the receiving process. Whenever the maximum number is exceeded, management takes corrective action to either speed up production at the receiving process or slow production at the previous process. This reestablishes the synchronicity and predictability of service production across the continuum.

5.6.2 Buffers

A buffer is a type of waiting area in which patients may be seen by the next process in a different order than the order in which they enter from the previous process. (See Figure 5.6b.) Buffers are appropriate whenever we are seeing patients whose diagnostic or treatment requirements differ significantly, and whenever patients may not be stable or their pain is not under control. For one reason or another, patients cannot be seen in the original order. Some of them need to get out of line. For obvious

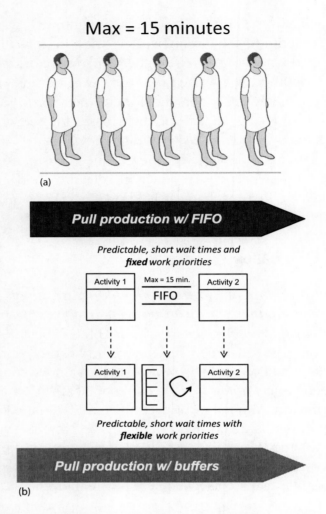

Figure 5.6 (a) Within a FIFO lane, patients must stay in their original order. The number of patients in a FIFO lane is controlled, as is the wait time. (b) Pull production with buffers combines flexibility with predictability.

reasons, buffers are appropriate for unscheduled services and especially for emergency situations. (See Figures 5.7 through 5.9.)

The number of patients in a buffer is determined in the same manner as for a FIFO lane, after making adjustments for the different cycle times associated with the different patient types accommodated in the continuum of care (acute and nonacute, male and female, old and young, scheduled and nonscheduled, and so on). To account for expected (and

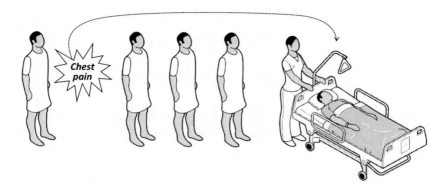

Figure 5.7 Within a buffer, the order in which patients are processed may vary.

Figure 5.8 A buffer before an emergency department. Which of the new arrivals will be served first?

Figure 5.9 This buffer protects flow in the hospital by freeing beds while patients ready to go home wait for transportation.

SUPERMARKETS

When buffers are applied to the storage and movement of medicines and supplies, they are referred to as *supermarkets*. The original idea for kanban occurred to the managers of the Toyota Motor Company during a visit to an American supermarket in the 1950s. They observed how an empty space on a shelf acted as a signal to restock the shelf with fresh product. This simple, visual system automatically synchronized the movement of product with the actual demand for that product. Courtesy of Toyota, supply systems throughout the world are now run as efficiently as American supermarkets.

unexpected) variation in process cycle times, buffers often make room for a few extra patients.

5.7 FLOW MANAGEMENT

In building a pull system, when we opt for a buffer instead of a FIFO lane, we often face the challenge that some patients are sicker than others and should be seen first. Sometimes, we know this information in advance and create schedules that establish the best order for dealing with patients, based upon their respective conditions. Other times, we may be confronted with emergencies, which by definition cannot be scheduled. One might think that emergencies would necessarily disrupt flow. In a flow, patients stay in a FIFO order; no one is permitted to get out of line. Of course, when an emergency occurs—when an ambulance arrives at the emergency department or when a patient's condition suddenly worsens in the intensive care unit—these patients deserve first priority. They go to the *head of the line* and disrupt the flow of other patients who must now wait to be seen.

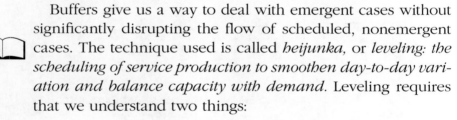

Buffers give us a way to deal with emergent cases without significantly disrupting the flow of scheduled, nonemergent cases. The technique used is called *heijunka,* or *leveling: the scheduling of service production to smoothen day-to-day variation and balance capacity with demand.* Leveling requires that we understand two things:

1. The frequency (i.e., the number we expect today) of emergent and nonemergent cases
2. The cycle times of emergent and nonemergent cases

If we understand these two things well enough, we can plan the flow of nonemergent cases, while leaving room, or extra capacity, in the schedule for emergent cases as they arise. The amount of extra capacity we need to build in is based upon historical demand and can be adjusted seasonally.

We must also have a mechanism to adjust the schedule in real time, as we learn more about the actual mix of emergent and nonemergent cases as it changes throughout the day. That

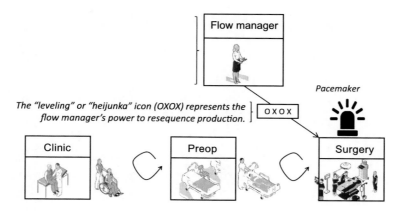

The "leveling" or "heijunka" icon (OXOX) represents the
flow manager's power to resequence production.

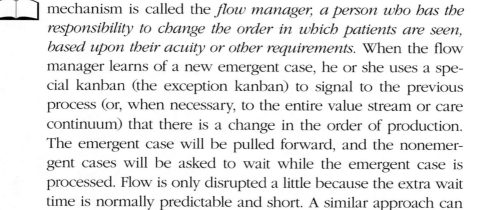

The patient is pulled by the next downstream process,
but only when it is ready to serve the patient.

Figure 5.10 The flow manager may resequence production at the pacemaker process, in real time, to reflect the changes in patient conditions or problems in operations.

mechanism is called the *flow manager, a person who has the responsibility to change the order in which patients are seen, based upon their acuity or other requirements.* When the flow manager learns of a new emergent case, he or she uses a special kanban (the exception kanban) to signal to the previous process (or, when necessary, to the entire value stream or care continuum) that there is a change in the order of production. The emergent case will be pulled forward, and the nonemergent cases will be asked to wait while the emergent case is processed. Flow is only disrupted a little because the extra wait time is normally predictable and short. A similar approach can be used to accommodate walk-ins and same-day appointments in outpatient clinics. (See Figure 5.10.)

TAKE FIVE

Take a few minutes to think about these questions and to write down your answers:

- Do you think your company's production schedule is closer to shish-kebob production or to leveled production?
- What would the average takt time be for the quantity of products your company produces each day?

5.8 IMPROVE THE PROCESS FIRST

Keep in mind that kanban is just a system for controlling the wait times of patients and the inventories of medicines and supplies. *If the processes themselves have not been improved to eliminate waste such as excess work in process, walking, conveyance, downtime, and defects, kanban will not work.* Chapters 4 and 6 describe key process improvement and standardization techniques that support the use of kanban and pull systems for just-in-time.

SUMMARY

Pull is a method for creating a system of production in which a downstream process producing to takt time signals to an upstream process that it is ready for the next patient, product, or other unit of work.

In a just-in-time system, it is essential that we

- Coordinate the movement of patients, clinicians, medicines, and supplies across the continuum of care—from one cell (or *island of flow*) to the next, and
- Synchronize that movement with the pace of service production in the cells.

To achieve this coordination, we can use kanban. Kanban are cards or other visual or electronic signals that indicate when a clinical cell or process is ready to see a patient, or ready for more supplies. The pacemaker process (usually the longest process) establishes the schedule or rhythm of service production.

In contrast, the traditional push production systems often used in healthcare depend on seeing patients, performing tests, and moving medicines and supplies according to separate, predetermined schedules. Often, these processes and their schedules are not linked together in a predictable or smooth way. Push systems tend to be unresponsive to changes in demand. Pull systems are very responsive to changes in demand, and they eliminate many forms of waste including waiting for care and excess inventory.

A typical kanban system uses four main types of kanban cards or devices:

1. *Production kanban:* Authorizes the previous process to see more patients.
2. *Rooming or restock kanban:* Authorizes a process to transfer patients, medicines, or supplies from the previous process.
3. *Move or supplier kanban:* Authorizes an outside supplier to deliver more medicines and supplies.
4. *Exception kanban:* Authorizes production, restocking, or movement in special recurring cases that may be difficult to anticipate.

There are five basic rules for the successful use of kanban:

1. Downstream processes signal to upstream processes when they are ready for the next patient.
2. Upstream processes do not send patients to downstream processes until they receive a kanban or signal; they begin to care for the next patient only once they have sent the last patient downstream.
3. All processes produce and deliver only 100% defect-free services to their patients or customers.
4. Service production is *leveled* across all processes, in order to synchronize it and prevent overproduction and waiting.
5. The kanban that govern the production of services for a patient tend to travel with the patient.

Pull systems employ two different mechanisms to ensure that wait times between service production cells are short and predictable: (1) FIFO lanes and (2) buffers. FIFO lanes are small areas where patients wait to be seen, in the same order in which they first entered the lane (that is, first-in-first-out). Buffers are waiting areas in which patients may be seen by the next process in a different order from the order in which they enter from the previous process. They are particularly helpful in situations where a patient may need to get out of line and be seen before another patient. The maximum number of patients in either a FIFO lane or a buffer is determined based on the travel time between cells or processes and the pace of production in the cells or processes involved. Whenever the maximum number is exceeded, management must take corrective action.

The technique we use to smooth out the production of services for different types of cases (e.g., emergent and nonemergent cases) is called heijunka, or leveling. Leveling requires that we understand two things:

1. The frequency (i.e., the number we expect today) of emergent and nonemergent cases
2. The cycle times of emergent and nonemergent cases

If we understand these two things well enough, we can plan the flow of nonemergent cases, while leaving room, or extra capacity, in the schedule for emergent cases as they arise.

The *flow manager* has the responsibility to resequence production at the pacemaker process, in real time, to reflect changes in patient conditions or problems in operations.

Successful use of pull and kanban requires that process improvements have been made to eliminate waste, such as excess work in process and defects.

REFLECTIONS

Now that you have completed this chapter, take a few minutes to think about these questions and to write down your answers:

- What did you learn from reading this chapter that stands out as particularly useful or interesting?
- Do you have any questions about the topics presented in this chapter? If so, what are they?
- What additional information do you need to fully understand the ideas presented in this chapter?

Chapter 6

Support Techniques for Just-in-Time

6.1 INTRODUCTION

This chapter describes several important techniques that support the smooth flow required for just-in-time (JIT) in healthcare. Additional information is available in the resources listed in the Appendix.

6.2 THE 5S SYSTEM FOR WORKPLACE ORGANIZATION AND STANDARDIZATION

The JIT approach cannot succeed in a clinic or hospital that is cluttered, disorganized, or dirty. Poor workplace conditions give rise to all sorts of waste, including extra motion to avoid obstacles; time spent searching for needed items; delays due to process interruptions; and increased risk of defects and harm to patients, clinicians, and staff.

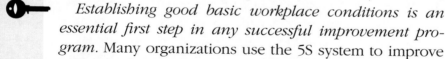
Establishing good basic workplace conditions is an essential first step in any successful improvement program. Many organizations use the 5S system to improve and standardize the physical condition of their work areas. (See Figure 6.1.)

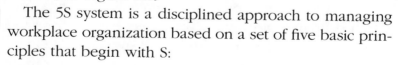
The 5S system is a disciplined approach to managing workplace organization based on a set of five basic principles that begin with S:

1. Sort
2. Set in order
3. Shine
4. Standardize
5. Sustain

Figure 6.1 The 5S system supports JIT and improvement in quality, safety, affordability, cleanliness, reliability, and access.

1. *Sort:* Teams of clinicians and support staff begin by sorting medicines, supplies, and equipment and removing any items that are not needed in the work area. They use a technique called *red tagging* to identify unneeded items and manage their disposition.

2. *Set in order:* Next, teams determine appropriate locations for items they do need. After relocating the items, they apply demarcation lines, labels, and signboards to indicate and maintain the new positions and quantities of tools, medicines, and supplies. The main idea is, "A place for everything, and everything in its place."

3. *Shine:* The third S involves conducting daily self-audits of each area using a tool called a *5-minute 5S checklist* to ensure that everything is always sorted and set in order. The third S also involves clinicians and

staff stopping to clean critical surfaces and equipment throughout the day to prevent hospital-acquired infections. In healthcare, cleanliness is too important to leave to the end of the day.

4. *Standardize:* In the fourth S, teams establish the new, improved conditions as a workplace standard that becomes second nature. At this stage, visual management methods are adopted to ensure that everyone in the workplace sees, understands, and can easily follow the new standards.

5. *Sustain:* The final 5S principle uses training and communication to maintain and monitor the improved conditions and to ingrain 5S into the work culture and spread 5S activities to other areas of the organization.

TAKE FIVE

Take a few minutes to think about these questions and to write down your answers:

- What physical conditions get in the way of doing the work in your area?
- What specific conditions would you change to make the work area easier to use?

6.3 VISUAL MANAGEMENT TECHNIQUES

Visual management of healthcare processes is an important support for JIT. For example, kanban cards are visual management tools that control when patients are seen and when medicines or supplies are moved to another process (see Chapter 5).

- *Visual management techniques express information in a way that can be understood quickly by everyone.*
- *Visual techniques help keep order in the workplace.* Lines, labels, and signboards (introduced in the discussion of

5S in Section 6.2) tell everyone, at a glance, where to find things, where to put them away, and how many should be there. (See Figure 6.2.) Using these methods to indicate locations and correct inventory numbers can help control costs, as well as eliminate a lot of time wasted in searching and replacing tools, medicines, and supplies.

- *Visual information can also help prevent mistakes.* Color coding is a form of visual display often used to prevent errors and defects. Where color blindness may be an issue, different patterns or icons can be used in addition to color, to identify what is what. (See Figure 6.3a and b.)

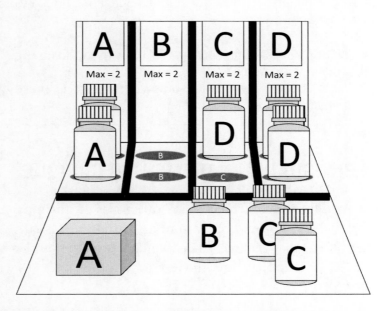

Figure 6.2 Visual management involves the use of lines, labels, and signs, as well as shapes and orientation, to help keep the right things in the right place in the right quantity. (Note that the box on the left labeled A will clearly not fit with the other supplies in this area, and one of the bottles labeled D is clearly misplaced in the C area.)

70

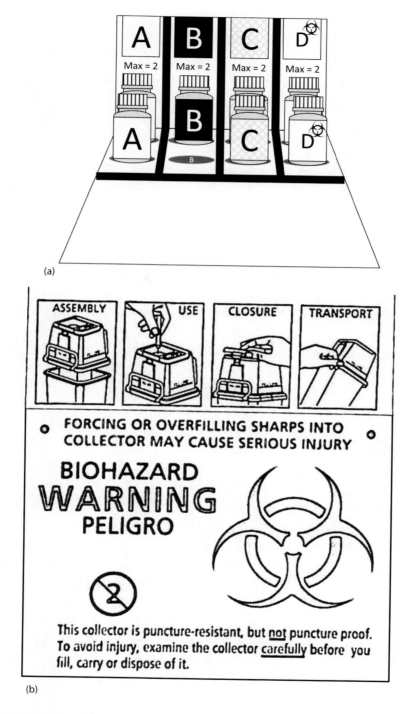

(a)

(b)

Figure 6.3 (a) Visual control can also be enhanced by the use of colors, patterns, and icons. (b) The biohazard icon on this sharps container is a form of visual control.

6.4 MISTAKE PROOFING

A mistake-proofing or *poka-yoke* system uses checklists or other devices to detect errors that could cause defects. *An error is something done incorrectly, through a misunderstanding or as a result of an unreliable or unstable process.* When not corrected, an error can result in *a defect, a nonconformance or departure from expected quality.*

The most effective mistake-proofing systems stop the process so that a defect cannot be made. Mistake proofing works by building the function of a checklist directly into the process. This gives the process a kind of memory so that clinicians and staff members, and even machines, are automatically reminded to do the job right. When a defect is made, it is easily discovered. Also, the process is stopped so that the defect is either prevented from occurring at all or prevented from being passed on to the next operation or process.

The key to effective mistake proofing is determining when and where defect-causing conditions arise and then figuring out how to detect or prevent these conditions, every time. Clinicians and staff on the front line of healthcare have important knowledge and ideas to share for developing and implementing mistake-proofing systems that check every patient and every procedure and give immediate feedback about problems.

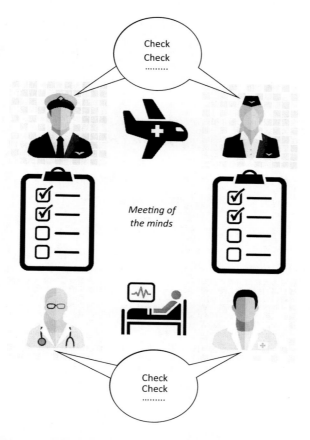

Figure 6.4   Checklists help to make processes mistake-proof.

6.4.1 Mistake-Proofing Checklists

 Where clinical risk is high and defects are simply not permissible, mistake proofing can be integrated into a process by using a checklist that requires two or more people to agree that the conditions required for quality and safety have been met. (See Figure 6.4.) This approach has been used for decades in the airline industry and has recently been introduced to healthcare in the form of the World Health Organization's Surgical Safety Checklist.

6.4.2 Zero Defects through Zero Quality Control

Mistake proofing is based on a quality system known as Zero Quality Control (ZQC). *Zero* refers to the goal of this approach: to make products and deliver services with zero defects. To experience zero defects is a basic expectation of the patient. Even one defect can cause serious harm to patients or staff, as well as patient dissatisfaction, rework, and higher costs.

The key to zero defects is to detect and prevent abnormal conditions before they can cause defects. ZQC is a defect-prevention system that uses inspection at the point where it can prevent defects—before the processing takes place.

ZQC combines four basic elements (see Figure 6.5):

1. It uses *source inspections*—a check for proper processing conditions—to catch errors before they become defects. It also uses *successive checks* (a check by someone in the succeeding process) and *self-checks* (systematic checking of one's own work against an appropriate standard).
2. It uses *100% inspection* to check all services, not just a sample.
3. It provides *immediate feedback*, thereby shortening the time for corrective action.
4. It uses poka-yoke (mistake-proofing) protocols and devices to check automatically for abnormalities when source inspections are not sufficient to achieve the required levels of quality and safety.

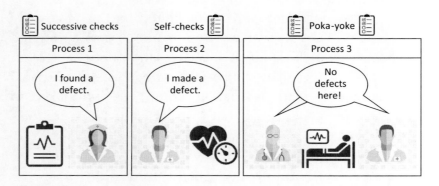

Figure 6.5 ZQC = source inspections, 100% inspections (including successive checks and self-checks), immediate feedback, and poka-yoke (mistake-proofing protocols and devices).

TAKE FIVE

Take a few minutes to think about these questions and to write down your answers:

- What kinds of actions or conditions can cause defects to happen in your process?
- Can you think of ways to *catch* these conditions before they result in defects?

6.5 QUICK SETUP METHODS

In healthcare, each patient is different. Special medicines, tools, supplies, and information often need to be produced or gathered before clinicians and staff can begin work. This work to prepare to serve the patient is called *setup*. Setup includes activities such as transporting, replacing supplies and equipment, preparing facilities, checking, and so on. Some healthcare operations, such as surgery, can be very complicated, involving multiple team members and specialized equipment and supplies.

To serve patients more effectively and economically, a health-care organization must learn how to reduce the time required for setups. Reducing setup times helps to improve access, safety, flexibility, and the ability to provide safe and appropriate care without mistakes or defects. The system for shortening setup time involves four stages, described in Sections 6.5.1 through 6.5.4. Using this approach, setups can often be reduced by 30% to 50%. With continuous improvement, even complex setups can be reduced to under 10 minutes and sometimes less, if not eliminated entirely. (See Figure 6.6.)

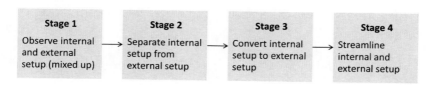

Figure 6.6 The four stages of quick setup.

6.5.1 Stage 1: Observe the Setup Process to Determine What Is Internal and What Is External to Setup

Internal setup refers to setup activities that

- *Must* be done after the previous patient has been seen, and
- *Must* be done before the next patient can be seen.

In other words, the process must stop for internal setup operations to be performed. Often, stoppage is required to ensure patient safety.

External setup refers to setup activities that either

- Can be done anytime before the next patient is seen, or
- Can even be done while the last patient is still being seen.

In most organizations, internal and external setup operations are jumbled together. This means that things that could be done while a process is running are not done until the process has stopped. Because in healthcare each patient often requires special setup operations, mixing internal and external setup leads to an enormous waste of value-added time and decreases the capacity of healthcare processes.

6.5.2 Stage 2: Separate Internal Setup from External Setup

Stage 2 involves sorting out the external setup operations so they can be done beforehand. This step alone can reduce setup time by up to 50%. Typical stage 2 activities include the following:

- Transporting the next patient and all necessary medicines, tools, and supplies to the work area while the previous patient is being seen
- Confirming the proper functioning of exchangeable equipment, tools, and supplies at the beginning of the day or before stopping the process

6.5.3 Stage 3: Convert Internal Setup to External Setup

The next step is to look again at activities done when the process is stopped—after the previous patient has been seen but before the next patient is seen—and to find ways to do them while the process is still running—while the previous patient is still being seen. Typical stage 3 improvements include the following:

- Preparing operating conditions in advance, such as assembling surgical kits with specialized tools.
- Reducing the number of vendors and the variety of tools and supplies.
- Standardizing evidence-based clinical practice to reduce the number of customized setups.

6.5.4 Stage 4: Streamline All Aspects of Setup

This stage chips away at the remaining internal and external setup time in several ways:

- Using parallel operations, with two or more clinicians or staff members working simultaneously.
- Using supplies that shorten setup times, e.g., switching from a disinfectant with a drying time of 10 minutes to one with a drying time of five minutes.
- Enhancing 5S to reduce time normally spent searching for and replacing supplies and equipment.

6.6 NEW MEASURES OF HEALTHCARE TARGET EXCELLENCE

 It is common wisdom that "what gets measured is what gets done." *To support JIT, it is crucial to use measures that reinforce the new way of operating.* Reliance on traditional measures such as labor utilization may make it hard to change. That is because efficiency in the traditional sense tends to keep clinicians and staff busy—frequently with non-value-added work such as overprocessing and overproduction—rather than focusing on the teamwork required to synchronize service production with demand.

Performance measures for JIT should not only recognize improvement but also show the remaining waste to be addressed. The following are some examples of performance measures that help motivate people to do the right things:

- *Value-added ratio:* This measure indicates how much of the total production lead time is spent in actual processing operations that transform and add value for the patient in terms of improved fitness, function, or information (see Figure 6.7).
- *Lead time (length of stay):* Healthcare organizations track the time elapsed, from the time that a patient is admitted to the time of discharge. Because so much of healthcare costs are costs of labor, shorter lead times are an important cost advantage. Combining

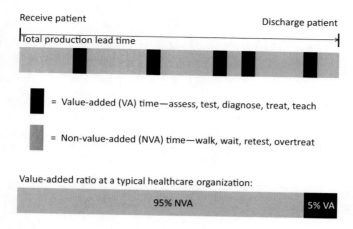

Figure 6.7 Value-added ratio.

lead time or the length of stay with the value-added ratio yields insights into the phases of production that need to be improved. Lead time reduction can also help improve access by improving throughput, leading to reduction in service backlogs, reduction in instances in which emergency rooms are put on diversion, and the prevention of patients from leaving without being seen.

■ *Inventory level:* The medicines, tools, equipment, and supplies used in healthcare are quite expensive. A JIT organization pays attention to the level of its raw materials to maintain the flow of care while using minimal *buffer* amounts in warehouses and storerooms. Inventories can be reduced by 50% or more in some cases. By reducing unneeded inventories, JIT also reduces instances where the needed medicine, equipment, or tool is *not* available.

■ *Setup time:* Quick setups are critical to flexible use of facilities, clinicians, staff, and equipment. They help level the schedule and create flexibility to see different types of patients and improve access for the organization's target populations.

■ *Patients or parts distance traveled:* This measure tracks the waste of moving patients or medicines and supplies between processes. A process-based layout should reduce this transport. (See Chapter 4.)

■ *Defect rate:* Zero defects is the goal, and not just in final inspection. Tracking defect rates for each process promotes mistake proofing and method improvement all along the continuum of care. (See Section 6.4 and Figure 6.5.)

TAKE FIVE

Take a few minutes to think about these questions and to write down your answers:

■ What kinds of measures are used at your organization?
■ What measures do you think are important to promote JIT in healthcare? To promote the morale of clinicians and staff? To promote patient satisfaction?

6.7 LEAN MANAGEMENT

 JIT *is not business as usual. Unsurprisingly, to be implemented and sustained, it requires a new approach to management. That new system is known as Lean management.*

 Lean management is the decentralized organization of management control structures to promote the discovery, correction, anticipation, and prevention of process defects and the errors and abnormalities that result in defects, patient waits, and other process delays.

In the broadest sense, Lean healthcare management can be explained in terms of five principles that define what we may call the DNA of Lean healthcare management:

1. Standard work
2. Autonomation
3. Flow production
4. Plan–Do–Check–Act (PDCA)
5. Socratic method

These five principles are summarized in Figure 6.8.

1. Standard work	All work should be organized as standardized sequences of standardized tasks performed within a standard time and supported by a standardized amount of work in process.
2. Autonomation	When defects occur, the process should stop until the defect is corrected. Where necessary, employ mistake-proofing checklists or devices to promote critical thinking about problems in the work.
3. Flow	Ideally, patients should flow through operations and processes without interruption and without waiting.
4. PDCA	When problems occur, they should be resolved *at the source* using the scientific method of PDCA (plan–do–check–act). "At the source" means close to where the problem originally occurred, which is normally far away from where it was eventually detected.
5. Socratic method	Leaders should employ the Socratic method of questioning to develop their people as scientific problem solvers.

Figure 6.8 The five principles of Lean management.

6.7.1 Standard Work

The first principle of Lean management is that all activity—whether clinical or administrative—is governed by means of standard work (see Chapter 4). *Standard work is defined as standardized tasks performed in a standardized sequence in a standardized amount of time and with a standardized amount of medicines, supplies, and equipment to support it.* Standard work has two functions. First, it reduces variation by bringing processes into statistical process control (i.e., the quality rate ≥ 3-sigma). When a process is in statistical control, the process has become predictable and we can stop fighting fires. Currently, most healthcare processes are significantly out of control at 2-sigma or probably lower. Second, standard work establishes controlled conditions for small tests of change using PDCA (see Section 6.7.4). Because controlled processes are predictable, we can concentrate on preventing defects in the future. For more information about standard work and how to implement it, see *Standard Work for Lean Healthcare* (2011).

6.7.2 Autonomation

The second principle of Lean management governs how different operations in a process are linked together. This principle is known as *autonomation* or, in Japanese, *jidoka. Autonomation is defined as stopping the process to build in quality.* Autonomation means essentially two things. First, we never send defects downstream to the next operation in the process; we must stop to fix defects immediately. Second, to increase the speed at which we discover and fix defects, we build inspection into each critical step of the process with checklists (such as the World Health Organization's Surgical Safety Checklist) and other mistake-proofing protocols and devices. (See Section 6.4.) In all handoffs from upstream to downstream operations and processes, there must be *zero ambiguity* about what the downstream operations and processes need from the upstream operations and processes that supply them.

6.7.3 JIT or Flow Production

The third Lean principle is flow production. *Flow means treating patients one at a time, with clinicians and support staff passing the patient from one step in the process to the next without inconveniencing him or her to wait or travel long distances.* Flow is always the most efficient way to deliver healthcare services. In flow, an operator (that is, a clinician or other staff member) completes work with one patient before proceeding with the next patient. A good example of flow in healthcare is the production of healthcare services for trauma victims. Flow can only happen when the downstream process serving the patient is ready. If the patient moves before that operation or process is ready, the patient will have to wait for the downstream operation. Flow is the natural outcome of eliminating the seven non-value-added wastes in Figure 2.1. It is the ideal state of an orderly production process. Flow happens in process-based layouts, the U-shaped cells described in Chapter 4.

Flow production has a corollary principle known as pull. If it is not possible for patients to flow through a healthcare process because of an acute medical condition or for any other reason, we will ask them to wait a short time, under the appropriate level of care, until the downstream process is ready to *pull* them (see Chapter 5).

6.7.4 PDCA

Chris Argyris, father of the learning organization concept, once described organizational learning as a process of detecting and correcting defects. One might say that a learning organization is an organization that finds defects and fixes them. A *Lean* organization is an organization that *anticipates* defects and *prevents* them through a process of what Argyris described as *double-loop* learning.* Single-loop learning is the repeated attempt to solve a problem, with no variation of method and without questioning the goal. Double-loop learning is the ability to modify organizational methods or even goals in the light of experience. *PDCA (also known as the Deming cycle or plan–do–check–act) is essentially the scientific method; it is the method by which double-loop learning is accomplished within the Lean enterprise.*

6.7.5 Socratic Method

The fifth and final Lean principle is the Socratic method. Lean processes are highly—some say *radically*—decentralized. To fix defects and maintain flow, clinicians and support staff must be both qualified and empowered to make decisions in real time. Otherwise, the time between the discovery and correction of defects will grow indefinitely as the permission to change

---

* For Argyris's comments about detecting and correcting defects, see M. Crossan. 2003. Altering theories of learning and action: An interview with Chris Argyris. *Academy of Management Executive* 17 (2):40. On double-loop learning, see Chris Argyris and Dan Schön. 1978. *Organization Learning: A Theory of Action Perspective.* Reading, MA: Addison–Wesley.

the process is chased up the chain of command. Obviously, this cannot be done without support from leaders, but that goes beyond management support in the traditional sense. In a Lean organization, leaders must be teachers who have mastered what is perhaps the most demanding and effective teaching method ever conceived: the Socratic method. Teachers (sometimes called *sensei*) use the Socratic method to encourage students to develop their own problem-solving powers by posing a series of open-ended questions rather than giving answers.

SUMMARY

Establishing good basic workplace conditions is an essential first step in any shopfloor improvement program. Many organizations use the *5S system* to improve and standardize the physical condition of their work areas. Using the 5S system, workplace teams sort and remove unneeded items, determine best locations for needed items, clean thoroughly, and then establish standards for maintaining improved conditions.

Visual management of the production process is an important support for JIT. Visual management techniques express information in a way that can be understood quickly by everyone. Lines, labels, and signboards can be used to indicate where to find things and where to put them away. Color coding, patterns, and icons can help prevent mistakes and make information easier to understand.

Mistake proofing to prevent errors and defects is also critical for smooth JIT production. The key to effective mistake proofing is determining when and where defect-causing conditions arise and then figuring out how to detect or prevent these conditions, every time. Checklists are used to help prevent errors and defects. ZQC combines four elements to catch all problems at the error or abnormality stage. We use successive checks and self-checks, as well as poka-yoke—mistake-proofing protocols and devices to check automatically for abnormalities.

Quick setup is essential for JIT in healthcare. Reducing setup times helps to improve access, safety, flexibility, and the ability to provide safe and appropriate care without mistakes or defects. The system for shortening setup time involves four stages:

1. Observe the setup process to determine what is internal setup (must be done after a patient is seen and before the next patient) and what is external setup (setup that can be done anytime before a patient is seen or while a patient is being seen).
2. Separate internal setup from external setup.
3. Convert internal setup to external setup.
4. Streamline all aspects of setup.

Using this approach, setups can often be reduced by 30% to 50%.

It is common wisdom that "what gets measured is what gets done." To support JIT, it is crucial to use measures that reinforce the new way of operating. Reliance on traditional measures such as labor utilization may make it hard to change because they don't focus on the teamwork required to synchronize service production with demand. Performance measures for JIT should not only recognize improvement but also show the remaining waste to be addressed.

Lean management, which involves decentralized management control structures designed to prevent errors and defects, is based on five key principles: (1) standard work, (2) autonomization, (3) flow production, (4) PDCA, and (5) the Socratic method.

REFLECTIONS

Now that you have completed this chapter, take a few minutes to think about these questions and to write down your answers:

- What did you learn from reading this chapter that stands out as particularly useful or interesting?
- Do you have any questions about the topics presented in this chapter? If so, what are they?
- What additional information do you need to fully understand the ideas presented in this chapter?

Chapter 7

Reflections and Conclusions

7.1 REFLECTING ON WHAT YOU'VE LEARNED

An important part of learning is reflecting on what you've learned. Without this step, learning can't take place effectively. That's why we've asked you at the end of each chapter to reflect on what you've learned. And, now that you've reached the end of the book, we'd like to ask you to reflect on what you've learned from the book as a whole.

Take a few minutes to think about the following questions and to write down your answers:

- What did you learn from reading this book that stands out as particularly useful or interesting?
- What ideas, concepts, and techniques have you learned that will be most useful to you during just-in-time (JIT) implementation? How will they be useful?
- What ideas, concepts, and techniques have you learned that will be least useful during JIT implementation? Why won't they be useful?
- Do you have any questions about the JIT approach? If so, what are they?

7.2 OPPORTUNITIES FOR FURTHER LEARNING

Here are some ways to learn more about JIT production in healthcare:

- Find other reference material on this subject. Several resources are listed in the Appendix.
- If your organization is already implementing JIT, visit other units or areas to see how they are applying the ideas and approaches you have learned about here.
- Find out how other organizations—particularly healthcare organizations—have implemented JIT. You can do this by reading about JIT and Lean in healthcare, by attending conferences and seminars, and by going on site visits and tours of Lean facilities.

7.3 CONCLUSIONS

JIT is more than a series of techniques. It is a fundamental approach for improving the production of healthcare services that benefits patients, clinicians, and staff. We hope this book has given you a taste of how and why this approach can be helpful and effective for you in your work.

APPENDIX

FURTHER READING ABOUT JUST-IN-TIME

Japan Management Association, ed. 1986. *Kanban—Just-in-Time at Toyota: Management Begins at the Workplace.* New York: Productivity Press. A classic overview; describes the underlying concepts and main techniques of the original just-in-time production system.

Ohno, Taiichi. 1988. *Toyota Production System.* New York: Productivity Press. Tells the story of the first just-in-time system, in the words of the Toyota vice president who was responsible for implementing it.

FURTHER READING ABOUT LEAN HEALTHCARE

Rona Consulting Group and Productivity Press, Thomas L. Jackson, series editor. **Lean Tools for Healthcare Series.** New York: Productivity Press:

- Jackson, Thomas L., ed. 2009. *5S for Healthcare.* Imparts the information needed to understand and implement this essential Lean methodology for organization in the healthcare workplace. Includes helpful how-to steps and practical examples.

- Jackson, Thomas L., ed. 2011. *Standard Work for Lean Healthcare.* Explains how standard work can be used in healthcare to improve patient safety and reduce costs. Describes work in terms of cycle time, work in process, takt time, and layout; illustrates how standardization can help establish best practices for performing daily work; and explains why it is the cornerstone for all continuous improvement efforts.

- Jackson, Thomas L., ed. 2012. *Kaizen Workshops for Lean Healthcare.* Describes what a kaizen improvement event entails and details the phases necessary to conduct a successful kaizen workshop in healthcare.

Covers planning, key roles, implementation, the presentation of results, and ongoing follow-up.

■ Jackson, Thomas L. 2013. *Mapping Clinical Value Streams.* Explains how to use the powerful value stream mapping process in healthcare to observe and depict clinical processes as they are, and to envision and configure them without waste. Defines value, value streams, and service families in clinical settings, and shows how to map the current state, discover opportunities to eliminate wastes and waiting, to create *flow* or *pull*, and to map your future-state processes.

■ Carlson, Samuel and Maura May, eds. 2016. *Mistake Proofing for Lean Healthcare.* Introduces the principles of mistake proofing in healthcare and explains how to build quality into processes in order to catch errors before they become defects. Includes examples of mistake-proofing (*poka-yoke*) methods and devices as used in healthcare.

Rona Consulting Group. 2015. *The Lean Healthcare Dictionary: An Illustrated Guide to Using the Language of Lean Management in Healthcare.* Defines essential Lean and healthcare terms to help create a common language for anyone involved in Lean healthcare improvement activities.

Graban, Mark. 2011. *Lean Hospitals: Improving Quality, Patient Safety, and Employee Satisfaction*, 2nd edition. Explains why and how Lean can be used to improve quality, safety, and morale in healthcare. Highlights the benefits of Lean methods and explains how Lean concepts can help identify and eliminate waste, to effectively prevent delays for patients, reduce wasted motion for caregivers, and improve the quality of care.

USEFUL WEBSITES

Lean Blog (http://www.leanblog.org)—A blog founded by author Mark Graban about Lean in hospitals, business, and our world.

Productivity Press (http://www.productivitypress.com)—The website of Productivity Press, where you may order the Lean Healthcare Series titles, *The Lean Healthcare Dictionary* (2015), and many other seminal and award-winning books about Lean, total quality management, and total productive maintenance.

Project Check (http://www.projectcheck.org)—Provides online access to various medical checklists.

Rona Consulting Group (https://www.ronaconsulting.com)—The official website of series editor Thomas L. Jackson and his partners at Rona Consulting Group (RCG). Provides many resources, including a blog featuring perspectives from the RCG team, articles, case studies, and management briefings.

World Health Organization (http://www.who.int/entity/patientsafety /en/)—Provides many valuable resources, including patient safety checklists with implementation and adaptation guidelines. For the surgical safety checklist, go to http://www.who.int/patientsafety/safesurgery /tools_resources/en/.

Index

Page numbers with f refer to figures.